" . . . he left his millions of readers the pleasure of adding their own details, light and shade to the characters he created, the situations he placed them in and the naturalistic, life-like dialogue he had them deliver."

ERNEST HEMINGWAY

An Illustrated Biography

David Sandison

HEMIN

NGWAY

Introduction

Although Ernest Hemingway had been caught, on at least two recent occasions, trying to use one of his many guns to bring an end to the confusion and misery into which debilitating illness, growing paranoia, electric shock therapy and an unyielding writer's block had cast him, no one had thought it prudent either to remove the arsenal from his home in Ketchum, Idaho, or at least render it harmless by hiding all the cartridges and bullets. It was an oversight which was destined to have a tragic outcome.

Early in the morning of Sunday, July 2, 1961, Hemingway crept quietly downstairs from the back bedroom he occupied, took a bunch of keys from the kitchen windowsill and made for a locked storage room in the basement. Selecting a British-made twelve-gauge Boss double-barrelled shotgun he'd bought some years earlier at Abercrombie & Fitch's New York sports store and sliding shells into its breech, he moved noiselessly back upstairs into a small foyer near the front door. Then, placing the cold muzzle against his head, Hemingway pulled the two triggers.

Upstairs in her bedroom, his wife Mary stirred awake at hearing what she later described as being like "the sounds of a couple of drawers banging shut." Deciding to investigate (she had already been up, at about 6 am, for a glass of water and noticed that Hemingway was moving about his room), Mary came upon a dreadful scene: "a crumpled heap of bathrobe and blood, the shotgun lying in the disintegrated flesh, in the front vestibule . . ."

The sight which greeted her was, by all reliable accounts, far worse than that. The upper half of Hemingway's head had been completely blown away. Fragments of flesh, hair, teeth and bones were spattered around the walls, floor and ceiling and Mary had been forced to step over some of this grisly debris on her way down the stairs. Her screams brought George Brown – a life-long friend and Hemingway's one-time boxing coach – running from an adjoining guest house. Brown telephoned Don Anderson, one of Hemingway's regular hunting companions, and it was they, aided by another hunting buddy, Lloyd Arnold, who tackled the grim task of cleaning up and burning the scattered fragments.

Understandably shocked, Mary was sedated and taken to a local hospital for an overnight stay even as all the leading news agencies sprang into action to inform a startled world that Ernest Hemingway, best-selling author, international celebrity, big-game hunter and larger than life Nobel Prize-winner, had died from gunshot wounds, probably self-inflicted, just 19 days short of his sixty-second birthday.

Mary Hemingway came out of hospital the next day fighting her corner. Her husband's wounds may have been self-inflicted, she conceded, but she did not believe that they were deliberately so. His death was nothing but a terrible accident. It was a story Mary would steadfastly and stubbornly repeat long after her husband's sad decline and

"No one had a right to deny a man access to his possessions."

previous suicide attempts had been revealed. Perhaps it was a line she had to maintain for her own peace of mind, for it was she who had decided not to remove or disable Hemingway's guns. Worse, it was also Mary who had left the keys to the basement out in plain view, something she would later try to justify by saying: "No-one had a right to deny a man access to his possessions."

Her protestations were aided hugely by the fact that Hemingway had left no suicide note, a fact which the Blaine County coroner seized on to avoid delivering a ruling as to whether the writer's death was accidental or intentional. No inquest was held because, under Idaho state law, none was required unless there was suspicion of foul play. Hemingway's own attitude to suicide was a key factor militating against his having killed himself, for he had long railed against his father's "cowardice" in taking that way out in 1928 when his investment portfolio took a dive.

As if to reinforce her protestations of accidental death, Mary Hemingway arranged for a local Roman Catholic priest, Father Robert Waldman, to conduct the burial service, despite the fact that

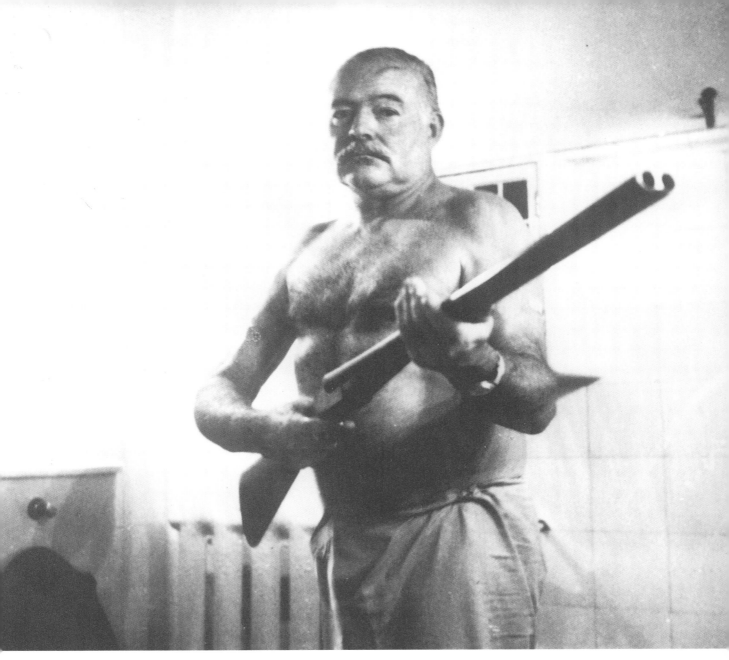

ABOVE Pictured with a weapon he used often in his life,
Cuba 1950

PREVIOUS PAGE Hemingway during some of the happier
times: a picnic with friends on Mazanares River, Spain, 1931

RIGHT A quiet moment, Malagar, 1959

Whether working as a reporter, novelist, essayist or short story writer, Ernest Hemingway had the ability to imply far more than he ever spelled out.

Hemingway, a convert to Catholicism, had been excommunicated after divorcing his second wife, Pauline, in 1940. Mary herself was not Catholic. If she reasoned that a Catholic funeral – which was never granted to a suicide – would help confirm that her husband's death was a bizarre accident, Mary Hemingway was only partially successful.

After taking advice from his superiors, Father Waldman did not perform the full requiem mass Mary had asked him to hold in his church. His compromise was to confine his ministrations to Catholic interment rites at the graveside ceremony held over until July 5, by which time Hemingway's sons had been contacted and had made their way to Ketchum – Patrick from Africa, Gregory from his studies at medical school in Miami, and Jack from Oregon, where he had been on a fishing trip.

It was the first time since the late 1940s that the three brothers had actually been together in the same place and, to the horde of international press and broadcast media reporters who watched the service from a respectful distance behind the cemetery's picket fence, they appeared to treat the event less as a cause for solemn grieving and more as an excuse to celebrate a pleasant reunion, exchanging smiles, laughter and jokes as they stood by a remarkably composed Mary. It was all very odd.

All in all, Ernest Hemingway's leaving of this world was every bit as fascinating and crammed with subtexts as any of the prose for which he had become justly lauded when his unique skills were at their peak. Whether working as a reporter, novelist, essayist or short story writer, Ernest Hemingway had the ability to imply far more than he ever spelled out in his carefully crafted and characteristically terse sentences, so leaving his millions of readers the pleasure of adding their own details, light and shade to the characters he created, the situations he placed them in and the naturalistic, lifelike dialogue he had them deliver.

As the literary world grieved voluminously at the death of a giant and irreplaceable talent and tributes poured in from others considered to be both great and good, Ernest Hemingway was laid to rest between two tall pines, his work done and his departure taken in a manner of his own choosing. Which was no more or less than the way he had lived his life – on his own terms, in his own style, and always in his own distinctive manner.

And it really had been a very remarkable life.

the

early years

(1899-1917)

A Midwestern Childhood

The family into which Ernest Miller Hemingway was born on July 21, 1899 was, in many ways, the epitome of the thrusting can-do society which created, built and transformed the fledgling United States during the 19th Century. The offspring of pioneering founding-father stock on one hand and tireless, ambitious and successful newcomer immigrants on the other, his parents considered themselves – with some justification – members of Chicago's upper class.

His mother, Grace, was the daughter of Ernest Miller Hall, a tall and distinguished English-born wholesale cutlery merchant whose family had emigrated from their native Sheffield, Yorkshire when he was in his teens and established a cattle farm near Dubuque, Iowa. In August 1861 – five months after the Civil War began when he was just 21 years old – Ernest Hall enlisted in the First Iowa Volunteer Cavalry, but was invalided out nine months later when a bullet smashed into his left thigh during a skirmish in Warrensburg, Missouri, leaving him incapable of riding.

Deciding to stress his Englishness, Hall dressed like a country squire, cultivated an imposing pair of muttonchop whiskers, and was habitually seen in the company of yapping Yorkshire terriers. As his cutlery business grew and thrived, Hall moved his family – wife Caroline and two children, daughter Grace and son Leicester – away from their first home on Chicago's South Side and into the more exclusive suburb of Oak Park, some ten miles west of the city. Across the way from them was the house of Anson Tyler Hemingway and his family.

A successful real estate entrepreneur, Anson was a descendant of Ralph Hemingway, a settler listed in a 1633 census as one of the freeholders then living in Roxbury, Massachusetts. Born in East Plymouth, Connecticut, in 1844, Anson was only ten years old when his family made the trek west to Chicago – where his father had been sent to open a new branch of a wholesale clock business – in a covered wagon. Like Ernest Hall, Anson Hemingway was a Civil War combatant, enlisting as a private in the 72nd Illinois Infantry in 1862. Promoted to the rank of lieutenant two years later, he helped recruit black infantry troops in Natchez, Mississippi before the war's end.

After studying at Wheaton College, Illinois, Anson Hemingway worked as General Secretary of the Chicago YMCA for ten years, during which time he became a friend of the evangelist Dwight Moody, Deacon of the city's First Congregational Church and a stalwart of the temperance movement. In time Anson also established his real estate business, sired four sons and two daughters, and bought the large family house at 439 North Oak Park Avenue where his first four grandchildren – Marcelline, Ernest, Ursula and Madelleine – would be born. It was his oldest son, officially named Clarence Edmonds but more commonly known as Ed, who would marry Ernest Hall's daughter, Grace, and become Ernest's father.

If Ernest Hemingway's two grandfathers had much in common as far as personal achievement and social standing were concerned, they

ABOVE The infant Ernest with his older sister Marcelline

differed in one important respect. While Ernest Hall was a man who had nothing but bad memories and a deep loathing of his Civil War experiences and (according to his grandson) forbade any mention of that conflict in his presence, Anson Hemingway revelled in his war memories, always marched (in full bemedalled uniform) in the annual Memorial Day parades, and encouraged the young Ernest to read and discover all he could about the war.

Perhaps more than anyone else, it was Anson Hemingway who instilled in Ernest the fascination with armed conflict, heroic deeds and heroes that he would retain throughout his life. In 1914, for example, Anson's Christmas present to Ernest was an inscribed copy of Lasalle Pickett's *The Bugles of Gettysburg,* while Ernest claimed to have been taken by Anson to see D.W. Griffith's 1915 movie *The Birth of a Nation* (replete with Civil War imagery) no less than 30 times. Anson also introduced Ernest to President Teddy Roosevelt – another veteran who never shrank from mention of his exploits, in his case during the Spanish-American War of 1898, when he led the fabled "Rough Riders" into action in Cuba – when he visited Chicago to work the hustings.

Ironically, in 1905, when the pacifist Ernest Hall decided to put an end to the agonies he was enduring during the last stages of the nephritis, which had atrophied his kidneys and reduced him to an anaemic wreck, he tried to do so with a pistol he kept under his pillow. Anticipating such a move, Ed Hemingway had removed the bullets – something the six-year-old Ernest considered a cruel act. And when, in 1928, Ed Hemingway elected to blow his brains out to avoid the disgrace of poverty, it was one of Anson's treasured Civil War pistols he used to perform the suicide of which Ernest was so disdainful and ashamed.

Hemingway's father was one of a distinctly odd couple who, despite appearing temperamentally mismatched, apparently made the very best of a marriage dominated by his wife's overwhelming conceit, bossiness, snobbery and pretensions. Perhaps it was the very oppositeness of their personalities which kept them together, for while Ed and Grace Hemingway did arrange for the occasional breathing space of separation (when Ed would go on lengthy "business trips'), they appear to have rarely had anything that qualified as a row – and certainly not within earshot of the children.

Ed Hemingway was a tall, hawk-nosed, bearded, tense, haggard and fussy man who struck Ernest's boyhood friends as gruff, formidable and somewhat forbidding. One of Ernest's female classmates has depicted Ed as having a "slightly seedy and unkempt air," putting that down to the fact that Grace Hemingway "never saw to it that he was well groomed, any more than she did her son."

A year older than his wife, Ed Hemingway first got to know her properly during his third year at Oak Park High School, and was immediately smitten by the buxom blue-eyed blonde with an impressive contralto singing voice. After high school graduation in 1890, Ed attended Oberlin College (from which he did not graduate) for three years before studying at Edinburgh University and Rush Medical College, from where he qualified in 1896. In time he would become

ABOVE Ernest, third from left, playing the pipe, with his sisters and Grandfather Hemingway on Decoration Day

medical examiner for three insurance companies and the Borden Milk Company, head of obstetrics at Oak Park Hospital (where he designed a new type of laminectomy forceps) and rise to the presidency of both the Oak Park Physicians Club and the Des Plaines Medical Society.

During what eventually became a very successful career, Ed Hemingway delivered more than 3,000 babies, including the six who would make up his own family: Marcelline (1898), Ernest (1899), Ursula (1902), Madelleine (1904), Carol (1911) and his second son, Leicester (in 1915). All were delivered at home, his wife supposedly convinced that Ed's hospital staff would mix her treasures up with other infants!

That fixation – and its subtle diminution of Ed's status and capabilities – seems typical of Grace Hemingway, a woman who was clearly spoiled as a child and would, when crossed, retire to her room with a hysterical headache. She found the ideal partner in Ed who, as a teenaged swain a-courting, promised that she would never be called on to do any housework if she pledged herself to him. He was as good as his word and, after they married, did all the grocery shopping, made the children's breakfasts (serving Grace's to her in bed), managed the household, its accounts and servants, and the catering when the family cook had a day off. This last-named chore was undoubtedly one born out of sheer necessity, for Grace's most notable culinary achievement was said to be a concoction of pork chops fried in cornflakes.

Grace was a paradigm of Oak Park society, which was invariably strait-laced, snobbish, strictly religious (firmly Protestant with a leaning towards Puritanism, as evidenced by the presence of only one Catholic church) and religiously "dry." As the Congregationalist minister, William Barton, described it, Austin Street – the thoroughfare which then marked the boundary between Oak Park and Chicago – was the point at which "the saloon stops and the Church steeples begin." Another Oak Park citizen at this time, architect Frank Lloyd Wright, would later characterize it wryly as "Saint's Rest" and describe its inhabitants as "good people . . . who had taken asylum there to bring up their children in comparative peace, safe from the poisons of the great city."

Grace's precocious vocal talents had looked set to bloom into a professional singing career, although her mother had balked at the suggestion that she study in Europe. The compromise solution, of a holiday in England and France followed by a year's tuition from a noted New York voice coach, Madame Capiani, climaxed in 1896 with Grace's debut at Madison Square Garden under the direction of Anton Seidl, principal conductor of the New York Philharmonic.

At that point Grace's story took a strange turn. Despite the fact that she was said to have received positively glowing reviews for this recital, Grace fled back to Oak Park and marriage to Ed Hemingway. She always claimed that her decision was enforced by the fact that stage lights hurt her eyes intolerably, although it is far more likely that she simply preferred the idea of being a big fish in a much smaller pond and was merely being realistic about her long-term career prospects. Back in Oak Park, however, Grace could be a celebrity, someone who had actually gone out into the big wide world and enjoyed a modicum of success. Her selfless sacrifice in "abandoning" her dreams of stardom for the sake of marriage and motherhood could – and would – be used as a weapon whenever Ed or the children dared question one of her imperious commands or displeased her in any way.

In her defence, it must be mentioned that Grace was said to have endured some months of blindness following a childhood bout of scarlet fever, a cause and effect unknown to medical science but one that nevertheless left her with a lifelong weakness she would pass on to her son in the form of the myopia and photo-sensitivity which made him unfit for military service. This particular inheritance would be one of the

LEFT Ed and Grace Hemingway with the family, Ernest top left, in a studio pose taken in 1909

long list of grievances Hemingway would cite to justify his hatred of Grace in later years, even though his father was extremely farsighted.

Although Grace heralded Ernest's arrival with a characteristically twee diary entry, which noted that "the birds sang their sweetest songs to welcome the little stranger to this beautiful world," there was never any doubt that Marcelline was, and would remain, the apple of her eye. It is also possible that she would have preferred to have given birth to another girl, for Ernest was destined to be dressed in lace-trimmed dresses and flowery bonnets and given a hairstyle identical to his sister's.

While this was common practice in many Victorian households, boys tended to be dressed as boys after no more than two or three years. Grace's son, however, had to suffer this indignity until he was four, was not given his first masculine haircut until he was six and was kept in short pants until he was 15. Amateur psychologists can make what they will of this as an explanation for Hemingway's later ferocious macho posturing, and he must have been mortified when fame inevitably led to the publication of old family photographs. Grace Hemingway also appears to have wished that Marcelline and Ernest had been born twins, since she arranged for Marcelline to be kept back a year at nursery school so that she and Ernest could embark on their full-time education at the same time.

When her father died, in May 1905, Grace Hemingway used her sizeable inheritance to build a grand new home – a 15-room, grey stucco and timber-trimmed house – at 600 Kenilworth Avenue. True to form, she had her architect design it so that its focal point was neither kitchen nor family sitting room but a huge music conservatory with a high ceiling and balcony. It was here that Grace ruled, either teaching her own or local children to sing and to play a variety of instruments (Ernest was forced to master the cello, eventually playing it in the high school orchestra) or holding the famed recital soirées of which she was inevitably the undisputed star.

Ed Hemingway had his own office–study, of course, but this lacked the Sioux Indian trophies – including the tomahawk and arrow heads he'd collected – which Grace calmly gathered up and burned on the day they moved into Kenilworth Avenue. Ernest, the only source of this story (which makes it suspect), would later claim to have been devastated by this act of wanton vandalism and amazed when, true to form, his father made no protest, even though he'd treasured those artefacts as mementoes of childhood expeditions with his own father, Anson.

Under grandfather Anson's proud gaze, Ernest threw himself into war and hunting games, a retreat from Grace's precious prissiness, and games made especially possible by the long summer holidays his family would take on Walloon Lake, in northern Michigan. Taken there for the first time when he was only seven weeks old, Hemingway would treasure the 20 vacations he eventually enjoyed in what must have been idyllic surroundings for a boy with a head full of Mark Twain's adventure stories, ready access to a fishing pole and, eventually and inevitably, his pick of real guns, both for sport and for securing family suppers. As contemporary snapshots show, Ernest shucked off his city clothes once in the country and dressed in Huck Finn fashion, resplendent in battered straw hat and buckskin trousers.

It was at Walloon Lake that Ed Hemingway and his son came closest to bonding. A victim of chronic hay fever in the city, Ernest's father found respite and refuge during the three summer months he habitually set aside for this annual vacation. The small cottage which he and Grace had built on the plot of land they purchased in 1900, named Windemere (sic) and enlarged as their family grew, was the place in which Ed Hemingway's savage soul could be revealed and indulged in an orgy of wildlife-slaying, remarkable even for those unenlightened times.

A caring physician and punctilious pillar of church and community back in Oak Park, Ed Hemingway felt duty-bound to transform himself into a rugged pioneer once the trek to Walloon Lake was completed and the groceries and household goods unpacked. Anything which flew, ran or swam was apparently fair game to Ed, who displayed a cheerful disregard for such niceties as official hunting seasons. Holy scripture decreed that God had given Man dominion over the earth, its riches and its creatures. Ed Hemingway, who enjoyed little or no dominion within his own household, elected to exercise that God-given right by trying to eliminate all the creatures that made their homes on and around Walloon Lake. It was an example his son was all too ready to follow, then and throughout his adult life, just as he was happy to accede to Ed's demands that he take up the noble art of boxing as soon as he was big enough to lace up a pair of gloves.

Ernest's keenness, and his impetuosity, would invariably lead to mishaps. The first of what would prove a lifetime of accidental injuries came at Walloon Lake when, running down a hill with a stick between his teeth, he fell, ramming the stick into his throat where it severed part of his tonsils. On another occasion he had to be rescued when a fishing hook lodged itself in his back – a painfully embarrassing way to learn how to cast a line properly.

He also followed his father's disregard of hunting rules and regulations by killing a protected blue heron in 1915. Aware that a game warden had discovered his crime, Ernest at first hid in the woods and then turned to his paternal uncle, George, for help. George refused, insisting that Ernest admit the offence and pay the fine, so gaining himself unsympathetic characterizations in a number of his nephew's short stories, most notably *Indian Camp* and *Three Shots,* where he appears, undisguised, as "Uncle George." His priggish rectitude during the heron incident would remain resolutely intact and when, in 1928, he refused to lend his brother the money which could have helped saved his bacon, George must have pushed Ed into the despair which led to his suicide.

Summer vacations also brought Ernest into contact, and something like friendship, with members of a local Indian tribe, the Ojibway. Although carrying the full weight of Oak Park prejudice – which would have unjustly categorized them *en masse* as feckless riff-raff – he envied the Ojibway their relaxed lifestyle and attitudes, drawing on his memories of them for the Nick Adams stories which he would begin writing in the 1920s.

BELOW The leisure and adventure of the wild – early days at Walloon Lake

The Oak Park High football team, with Ernest seated second from right in the front row

These contain numerous references to the young Nick's awakening sexuality, something their creator undoubtedly experienced during his teens at Walloon Lake when one of his companions was a young Ojibway girl, Prudence Boulton. Although Ernest's younger sister, Sunny (Madelleine), claimed she "never saw any evidence of Ernie's liking her or even wanting her along on our exploring trips," Prudence was to appear in two Nick Adams tales, her real identity scarcely veiled by the aliases Hemingway gave her. She appeared as Prudence Mitchell in *Ten Indians* (when she breaks Nick's heart by being caught in *flagrante delicto* with another boy), and as Trudy Gilby in *Fathers and Sons* (when she initiates Nick into the joys of sex, the first time with her brother present). She and the young Ernest may not have actually been sexually intimate, but there is no doubt that his teenage fantasies of Prudence remained potent for many years.

Just as potent – and one good reason for supposing that Ernest's relationship with Prudence did remain platonic – were Ed Hemingway's dire warnings concerning the dreadful fate awaiting any young man who strayed from the straight and narrow. Subsequently translated into Nick Adams' memories of his own father's strictures in *Fathers and Sons*, "masturbation produced blindness, insanity and death, while a man who went with prostitutes would contract hideous venereal diseases and that the thing to do was to keep your hands off of people."

If Ernest and Ed were generally as one at Walloon Lake, they differed greatly in one important respect: Ed considered any solitary occupation, especially reading, a complete waste of time. Far better to be doing something, anything, than indulging in such a pointless activity. To a boy who was increasingly engrossed and enthralled by words, and their power to create vivid thrilling images in his head, this was both intolerable and inexcusable. Ed Hemingway was set firm, however, even ordering the family nurse to remove all books from Ernest's room last thing at night. Necessity being the mother of invention and guile, Ernest simply created a number of hiding places to ensure that his voracious ingestion of literature could continue.

Genesis of a Writer

That love of words, and his own attempts to express himself, finally blossomed during Ernest's last few years at Oak Park High School, thanks in no small part to the encouragement and inspiration he received from two English teachers, Margaret Dixon and Fannie Biggs. In some respects, his senior high school career seems to have been devoted as much to extra-curricular activities as it was to academic studies – he competed in the football, swimming and water polo teams, boxed, managed the athletics squad, played in the orchestra, took a leading role in the senior play (a production of *Beau Brummel*) and joined the debating society. Nevertheless, his senior-year grades in English, algebra, law and history were rated exceptional, good for chemistry and zoology, and average in geometry and Latin.

His appointment as editor of Trapeze, the school newspaper, coincided with the appearance of his first three short stories in the pages of Tabula, Oak Park High's magazine. Although necessarily juvenile, they displayed precocious confidence and a heavy debt to tales by Jack London, Rudyard Kipling and O. Henry, increasingly influential elements of Hemingway's ferocious reading habits. Kipling was to remain a life-long soul companion, as his poems and stories were a continued source of inspiration to Hemingway, who would also read them to his sons as they grew up.

Influential too, was the Chicago Tribune sports writer Ring Lardner, and it was his snappy, colloquial style which Hemingway and his cohorts copied to give Trapeze a distinctive voice. By now Hemingway had

Vol XXIII   Oak Park, Ill., November, 1916   No. 1

adopted the nickname "Hemingstein," an early example of the many alternatives he preferred to the more soppy Ernest, and which had begun with Wemedge, Taty and Stein, and would continue until he settled on the suitably patriarchal Papa. He also liked to give his friends nicknames, another habit he maintained through the years.

Editing Trapeze fixed Hemingway's ambitions firmly on a career in journalism, despite his parents' often-stated wishes that, like his father, he attend Oberlin College and study medicine. His dream of joining the growing number of Americans who were volunteering for action in the world war that had been raging since 1914 – but which the United States had not entered until April 1917 – was effectively vetoed by Ed's opinion that he was too young. Instead, Hemingway found himself headed for Kansas City and a trainee reporter's job with that city's illustrious newspaper, the Star, thanks largely to a friendship his uncle, Tyler Hemingway, shared with its chief editorial writer, Henry Haskell.

It was in October 1917 that Ernest Hemingway was seen off by his father in a faintly embarrassing and emotional railway station scene he would use to great effect in *For Whom The Bell Tolls* when Robert Jordan's own memories of his home-leaving and his father's moist eyes, made him feel "suddenly so much older than his father and sorry for him that he could hardly bear it."

As his train headed south-west towards Kansas City, Ernest Hemingway was embarking on what would prove far more than a first break with the stuffy, claustrophobic atmosphere of Oak Park and an introduction to the hurly-burly of life as a cub reporter in a rumbustious, fast-moving city. It was a full and final end to everything he'd known in his first 17 years and the beginning of an adventure destined to make him one of the world's most famous figures.

ABOVE The first issue of Tabula, the Oak Park High School magazine, in which Hemingway had three short stories

RIGHT Ernest being congratulated by his father on the day of his High School graduation

war

and love (1917–1921)

Kansas City

Kansas City was everything Ernest Hemingway had dared imagine it would be. A sprawling and fast-growing metropolis, it still boasted a frontier town atmosphere, thanks largely to its role as terminus for both the Santa Fe and Oregon cattle trails and its position straddling both the great Missouri River and the boundary that separates the states of Kansas and Missouri – all of which combined to make the city a hectic and thriving port and marketplace for the vast agricultural riches amid which it nestled. Oil refining and heavy manufacturing industry would be added to make the city first settled by French fur traders in 1821 – and only granted a town charter in 1889 – an enervating place in which to be a young journalist hungry for experience.

Destined to provide Hemingway with much material for later stories, Kansas City was also to prove a fabulous training ground, thanks to the type of prose favored by the Kansas City Star, whose style handbook demanded short, precise sentences and paragraphs, precision, clarity and immediacy from its writers. Described later by Hemingway as "the best rules I ever learned for the business of writing," that particular style would form the foundation of all his subsequent work.

After a few weeks living with his uncle's family, which all too much resembled life in Oak Park, Hemingway moved to share a small attic rented by Carl Edgar, an acquaintance he'd first met at Walloon Lake. Fated, like so many others, to be portrayed in one of Hemingway's Nick Adams stories (in *Summer People* he is described as ". . . awfully nice. He had been nicer to Nick than anybody ever had"), Carl worked for a fuel oil company. Paid $60 a month for his work on the Star, Hemingway's share of the rent – including two meals a day – was $35 a month.

While not well off financially, Hemingway soon became rich in experience, thanks to his being given the "short-stop run" – covering crime stories in the police station, the hospital (where he checked on accidents, deaths and the aftermath of violent crimes) and the railway station (another mine of good stories and contacts and the occasional travelling celebrity). Developing a brash veneer in order to cover the polite reticence drummed into him during childhood, he liked nothing more than riding in police cars and ambulances as they raced through the city streets, although he often balked at asking interviewees for details he considered too personal.

More interested in writing features than hard news items, Hemingway was most proud of a piece called "Mix War, Art and Dancing" which recounted the tale of a woman excluded from a society dance. It was left to the reader to work out that the woman was actually a prostitute – Hemingway only laid clues, omitting details deliberately in precisely the same way he would in his later prose.

A number of Hemingway's stories for the Kansas City Star (many uncredited at the time, but identified and reprinted later) display a keen interest in the same subjects which would later dominate his fiction – violence and heroism, death and suicide, crime and sport, especially

LEFT Hemingway in his Section 4 ambulance, 1918

PREVIOUS PAGE Ernest on a canoeing trip, in Des Plaines, Illinois, off Lake Michigan in 1917

boxing. It is no accident that several of those stories dealt with military recruitment, for he was growing ever more determined to catch some of the action in Europe before the war burned itself out.

A new friendship, with another Star journalist, Ted Brumback, only served to fix Hemingway's determination. Brumback, a Kansas City judge's son, had been accepted by the American Field Service and had driven an ambulance in France from July to November 1917, despite having lost an eye in a golf accident. Already rejected by the U.S. military because of his own defective eyesight, Hemingway seized on this back-door chance, applied to the American Red Cross in December and, to his delight, was readily accepted.

Hemingway's War

On April 30, 1918 Hemingway left the Star, travelling immediately to New York where he was commissioned as a second lieutenant in the Red Cross and took part in a grand parade reviewed by President Woodrow Wilson. Before sailing from New York on May 23 aboard the *SS Chicago,* a French-line merchant ship rumored to be used by German spies and therefore presumed safe from attack by the Kaiser's submarines, Hemingway created uproar in Oak Park by solemnly informing his parents and friends that he had become engaged to Mae Marsh, a movie actress who had starred in D.W. Griffith's epics *The Birth of a Nation* and *Intolerance.*

The engagement was, of course, a hoax, but it threw Hemingway's parents into a turmoil. His mother wrote a tear-stained letter asking: ". . . You may come home disfigured and crippled; would this girl love you then?" Forced to wire home an admission of his ill-considered joke, Hemingway received a furious reply from his father which claimed that Grace had endured five nights' broken-hearted sleeplessness.

Sleep was the one thing Hemingway was not deprived of during the week-long voyage to Bordeaux, most of which he and Ted Brumback (who'd decided to return for another tour of duty) appear to have spent playing cards or dice. Travelling on to Paris, they arrived during a bombardment from massive German guns based some 100 km away near Amiens. This was an indiscriminate barrage born out of desperation as the Allies rebuffed Germany's last infantry offensive and which only served to blow pieces of masonry about and force the city's citizens into underground shelters.

Hemingway was not about to be driven under cover. Scenting the chance to wire a dramatic first-person story back to the Kansas City Star, he and Ted Brumback asked a taxi driver to take them to where shells were falling. After an hour they had the thrill of seeing a German shell hit the front of the Madeleine church, even if the damage was slight.

Ordered to take up his first posting in Milan, Hemingway had something of a baptism of fire. The day he arrived coincided with an explosion in a nearby munitions factory and he found himself detailed to helping extinguish a fire which had spread to a field outside the

ABOVE Ernest practising his gunmanship while on active service in Italy

compound, and carrying the mutilated bodies and dismembered limbs of workers to an improvized mortuary. He was horrified to discover that many of these were women.

Moved on two days later to an ambulance unit based at Schio, about 60 km east of Lake Garda, Hemingway spent three frustratingly boring weeks there, which were only enlivened by his writing a Ring Lardner parody for Ciao, the unit's newspaper, and meeting John Dos Passos, the Harvard graduate son of a wealthy Chicago lawyer of Portuguese descent. Like Hemingway, Dos Passos was hunting thrills and spills as an ambulance driver. Unlike Hemingway, who would nevertheless become a good friend, he would recoil from the brutality he witnessed, finding no merit in conflict. His first novel, *Three Soldiers,* published in 1921, was an unashamedly anti-war polemic.

Wanting to get closer to the "real" war, the point at which Italian and Austrian forces confronted each other, Hemingway volunteered to run a Red Cross canteen in north-east Italy, on the Piave front. His initial frustration at being restricted to running a *posto di ricovero,* dispensing chocolate and cigarettes to the wounded and front-line soldiers, would be recalled vividly in the Nick Adams story, *A Way You'll Never Be,* and give Hemingway's alter ego a chance to rail at the indignity of being a token – and strictly non-combatant – Yankee in the midst of men who understandably, though mistakenly, took his presence as proof that American reinforcements were about to arrive.

Hemingway got his glimpse of the reality of war at midnight on July 8, 1918, at Fossalta di Piave. He was handing out comforts in a trench when an Austrian mortar shell – a crude oil drum-like device packed with explosives and scrap metal – exploded only a metre or so away, instantly killing the man who stood between him and the blast. Hemingway himself was severely wounded in the legs by flying shrapnel and knocked unconscious by the blast. When he came to, and despite having 237 separate wounds in his legs, he managed to pick up and carry a badly wounded soldier some distance to a first-aid post. It was then that he realized the extent of his own injuries and allowed himself to be placed on a stretcher before passing out again.

It was only after he'd been carried three kilometres, and waited two more hours in a stable for an ambulance, that Hemingway was given morphine and tetanus shots before having almost 30 fragments removed from his legs. The pain must have been unbearable throughout, but his own first full account of the episode – given in a letter to his family just over a month later – claimed that his injuries: ". . . didn't hurt a bit at the time, only my feet felt like I had rubber boots full of water on. Hot water. And my knee cap was acting queer . . . We took off my trousers and the old limbs were still there but gee they were a mess. They couldn't figure out how I had walked 150 yards with a load with both knees shot through and my right shoe punctured in two big places . . ."

However, not included in that letter home was Hemingway's later claim that he had also suffered two wounds to his scrotal sac and was forced to rest his thankfully intact testicles on a pillow once he was moved from a field hospital in Fornaci to a Red Cross base hospital in

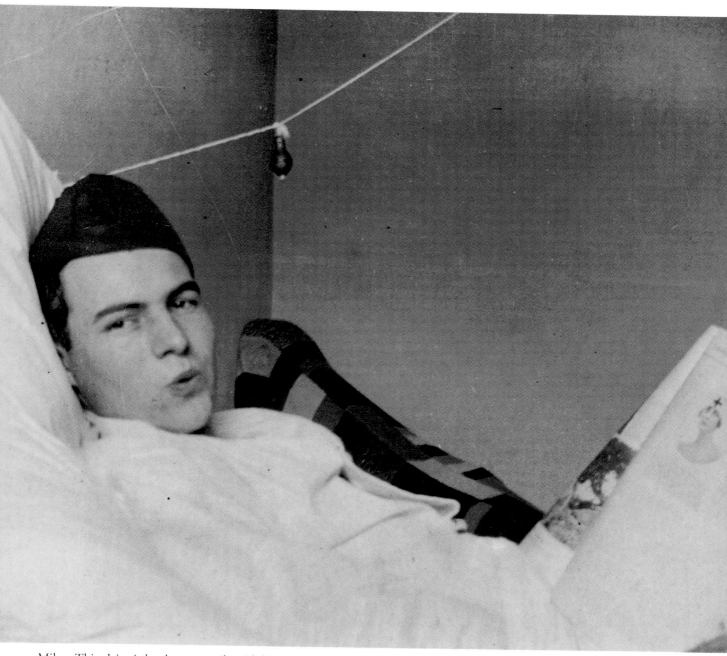

Milan. This claim is hard to reconcile with his account of making love with Agnes von Kurowsky, the Red Cross nurse assigned to look after the 18-year-old hero during his treatment and convalescence there, unless he was indeed a very fast healer!

What is not in doubt is the fact that Hemingway would have found himself in the company of men who had suffered genital mutilation, or worse. As ever, their agony – and the implications such injuries had for them in later life – would provide grist for the Hemingway word-mill. Although not explicitly described, it would be a similar wound which so blighted and scarred Jake Barnes in *The Sun Also Rises,* while Hemingway's own memories of the explosion which almost claimed his life would be used in almost precise detail to describe Frederic Henry's experience in *A Farewell To Arms.*

The extent of Hemingway's physical injuries are confirmed by official reports of the time, while his undoubted bravery was to be rewarded with the Italian Medaglia d'Argento al Valore, the citation for which said: "Gravely wounded by numerous pieces of shrapnel from an enemy shell, with an admirable spirit of brotherhood, and before taking care of himself, he rendered generous assistance to the Italian soldiers more seriously wounded by the same explosion and did not allow himself to be carried elsewhere until after they had been evacuated."

Bill Thorne, a Red Cross colleague and Hemingway's good friend, explained: "The Italians were pretty generous with the Croce di Guerras; I have three, I think. But they were damn tough and tight about awarding the Medaglia d'Argento al Valore . . . you had to be damn near killed, in a most honorable way, to get that."

Typically, Hemingway juggled the severity of his experience at Fossalta di Piave, sometimes exaggerating his wounds and bravery, at other times subsiding into rare displays of stoic modesty. Apart from incorporating aspects into his fiction, he would also use a description of the event to great effect in 1937, when he addressed a gathering of Hollywood's *creme de la creme* at a screening of his film documentary, *The Spanish Earth,* staged as a fundraiser to buy ambulances for Loyalist forces embroiled in the Spanish Civil War.

You could have heard a pin drop as Hemingway pleaded his cause, explaining that – in the early stages of injury – it was "not very painful . . . more like being knocked down by a club . . . But in about half an hour, when the shock has worn off, the pain starts and when the pain really gets going, you will truly wish you were dead if the ambulance is slow in getting there." Hemingway, remember, had waited many hours for the ambulance that had carried him away for proper treatment, and everyone present at the screening knew that.

Agnes von Kurowsky

Ernest Hemingway was not the first young man – and definitely not the last – to fall head over heels in love with the beautiful nurse who guided him through the darkest days and nights of slow recovery from serious injury. But his fixation with Agnes von Kurowsky was to be all-consuming and – when she finally declined to marry him – provide a rich source of inspiration both for the bitter-sweet scenario of *A Farewell to Arms* and the character of Catherine Barkley, the English nurse doomed to die in childbirth after her affair with Frederic Henry, the young American lieutenant wounded, just as Hemingway had been, in service with the ambulance corps in Italy.

Quite how all-consuming that fixation became was discovered in July 1961, after his suicide. Prominent among the documents and personal effects in Hemingway's study was a bundle of letters from Agnes. Forty years after she had jilted him, through four marriages, innumerable affairs and countless addresses, Hemingway had preserved those fragmented memories of his first great unconsummated and unrequited love.

LEFT Agnes von Kurowsky on duty at the Red Cross hospital

Seven years older than her patient, Agnes was born in Germantown, Pennsylvania, the daughter of a German-born father and an American mother from a distinguished military family. A fluent French speaker, Agnes had spent her early years on army posts in Vancouver and Alaska and had also worked as a librarian in Washington DC before training as a nurse in New York. Tall, slim, with chestnut hair and blue-grey eyes, she was characterized by Henry Villard, a fellow patient who would collate, edit and publish her diaries in 1989, as "easily the most scintillating of the nurses . . . cheerful, quick, sympathetic, with an almost mischievous sense of humor."

Volunteering for night duty in order to spend more uninterrupted time with the big, good-looking patient whom she would later describe as "always in good spirits, despite the severity of his wounds," Agnes was to find herself drawn inexorably to a quite remarkable, and remarkably brave, young man. She recalled how, terrified that his doctors might decide to amputate his leg, and determined to eliminate any possible source of gangrene, Hemingway resorted to drastic measures: "The first few days, he was using a pen knife to dig out pieces of shrapnel. He was still doing it when he got home, he said in a letter."

More ominously, especially considering Hemingway's later alcoholism and drink-related illnesses, Agnes also recalled that "he drank brandy all the time. I think he slept very well." If he did sleep well, it was without Agnes, who vehemently denied and clearly resented all later assumptions that, as the character of Catherine Barkley was so clearly based on her and that of Frederic Henry so obviously based on Hemingway's dream of himself as war hero – they had been lovers in real life.

Until her own death, in 1984, Agnes would protest that while she had loved Ernest Hemingway, she had never made love with him. That commitment was being saved for when he returned to America, found himself a job and sent for her. Then they would be married and only then would they sleep together.

It did not, of course, happen that way. After Hemingway returned home, Agnes met and fell in love with Lt. Domenico Caracciolo, heir to a Neapolitan dukedom. Before she learned that his family would not permit marriage to a woman they viewed as no more than an upstart American gold-digger, Agnes wrote Hemingway a curt, regretful letter which he (again drawing on life for his fiction) would refer to in his novella *The Snows of Kilimanjaro*.

There, his central character, Harry, described the effect rejection by a former lover had had on him: "He had written her, the first one, the one who left him, a letter telling her how he had never been able to kill it [his love] . . . How everyone he had slept with only made him miss her more. How what she had done could never matter since he knew he could not cure himself of loving her."

If Harry was only articulating Hemingway's own deepest thoughts, they go a long way to explaining his repeated failure to sustain any of his four subsequent marriages and his many brief and inevitably stormy love affairs. Indelibly scarred by Agnes' betrayal, he could never trust any woman completely and would cause all relationships to collapse beneath

ABOVE Agnes and Ernest in the grounds of the base hospital

the weight of his paranoia. No matter how loving or loyal his women were, Hemingway's innate mistrust was calculated to drive them away. It was a self-fulfilling prophecy he would repeat time and again.

After an idyllic summer of sightseeing in and around Milan (which included trips to the La Scala opera house, the medieval majesty of the Duomo, Europe's third largest church, the more secular delights of horse races at San Siro, as well as carriage rides in the city and the surrounding countryside), Hemingway and Agnes also made a trip to Stresa, on Lake Maggiore, in September. It was there that he met – and absorbed details about – Count Greppi, a distinguished 100-year-old former diplomat who would be transformed into the character of Count Greffi in *A Farewell to Arms*.

Early in October, Agnes was posted to Florence for two months – and to Treviso in December – while influenza epidemics raged. Bored and eager to return to the front, Hemingway persuaded his superiors to allow him to join an ambulance detachment just as the Italian army was launching its final victorious offensive against the Austrians at the battle of Vittorio Veneto, north of Venice. Arriving with the fighting at its height, Hemingway immediately realized that it was all too much for him in his still-frail condition and returned to Milan.

Hemingway's fantasies (or lies, if you prefer) about his wartime exploits conveniently omitted this humiliating retreat. As early as January 1919 he was telling newspaper readers back home that he'd stayed at the front until the armistice, on November 11. A form he completed for the Oak Park American Legion claimed that he'd served as a first lieutenant in the 69th Infantry division of the Italian Brigata Ancona during the Monte Grappa offensive in October-November 1918, while he muddied historical waters to assert on many other occasions, and with a vehemence which only added credibility to his version, that he'd also seen service with the Arditi, the corps of courageous almost suicidal volunteers that would form the core of Benito Mussolini's Fascist squadrons in the 1920s.

The last time Hemingway and Agnes von Kurowsky were together was on December 9, 1918, in the town of Treviso, although the regular, almost daily correspondence between them would continue until March, when she wrote to announce her "engagement" to Domenico Caracciolo. Before that, and immediately prior to his triumphant return home as a decorated war hero, Hemingway accepted the offer of Jim Gamble, an heir to the Procter & Gamble empire, to spend Christmas week at the older man's villa in Taormina, on the east coast of Sicily between Messina and Catania.

This would, in many ways, prove a pivotal event in the young Hemingway's life. For one, Gamble offered to become his patron, funding a year's travel in Italy. It was a generous offer, but one which came with a proviso – Gamble was to accompany Ernest throughout this sojourn, and there was little doubt that his interest was not entirely platonic. Although Agnes would claim that it was her advice that helped decide Hemingway against accepting Gamble's proposal ("I told him he'd never be anything but a bum if he started traveling around with somebody else paying all the expenses"), a passage in *Death in the Afternoon* is more revealing of Hemingway's motives for heading home:

"The friend, who was a little older, he had met only recently, but they had become great friends and he had accepted his friend's invitation to come abroad as his guest. His friend had plenty of money and he had none and their friendship had been a fine and beautiful thing until tonight. Now everything in the world was ruined for him."

Fleeing Gamble's unwanted advances, Hemingway began the long trek back to Oak Park early in January, leaving from Genoa and crossing a storm-tossed Atlantic after a three-day stay in Gibraltar before finally reaching home at the end of the month. He did so having acquired a new friend whose companionship during many adventures in Spain, Italy, Switzerland and Germany between 1919 and 1925 would leave a deep and lasting impression on the young American.

Hemingway met Captain Eric Edward "Chink" Dorman-Smith at the Anglo-American Club, Milan, on Italian Armistice Day, November 3, 1918. A temporary major and commanding officer of the Fifth Northumberland Fusiliers, Chink was a graduate of the Royal Military College at Sandhurst, had seen his first war action at Mons, had commanded a battalion at Passchendaele, been wounded three times and won the Military Cross for conspicuous gallantry under fire at Ypres. The son of an Irish Catholic squire, he was tall, thin, black-haired and blue-eyed. He was also a witty and intellectual charmer who immediately nicknamed the Anglophile Hemingway "Popplethwaite."

RIGHT Hemingway on crutches during his recovery at the Milan American Red Cross hospital

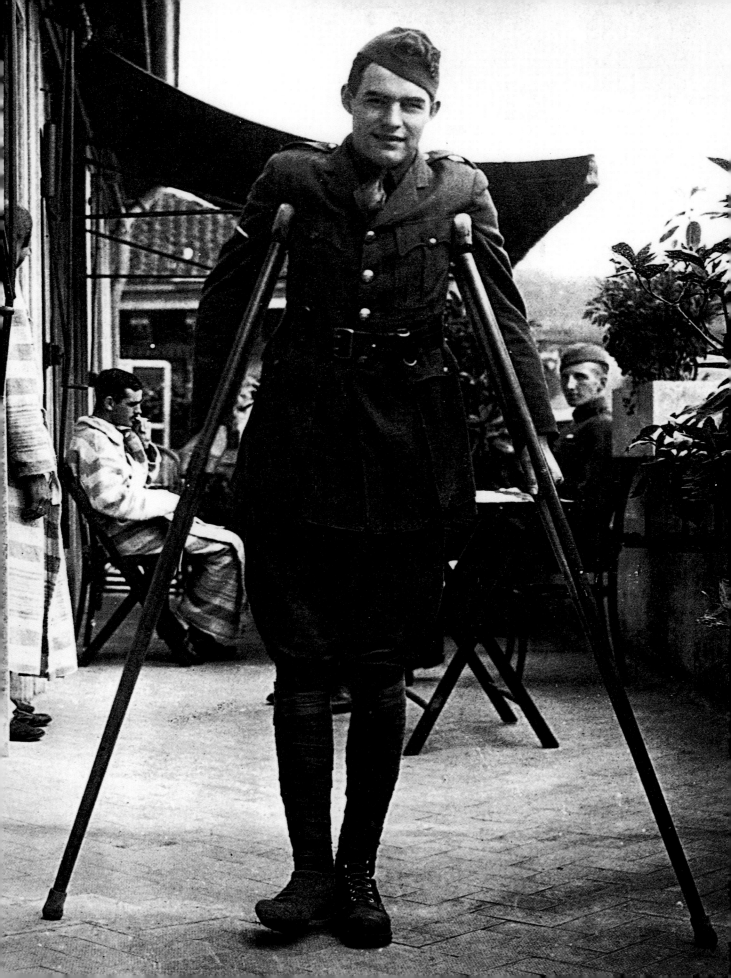

Their friendship blossomed despite some of the improbably tall tales of derring-do with which Hemingway filled their early alcohol-fuelled evenings together – when the claims of service with the Arditi first emerged and his stay with Jim Gamble became fancifully transformed into a week locked in the nymphomaniacal embrace of a Sicilian hotel hostess. Dorman-Smith would become godfather to Hemingway's first son, John, and something of a hero to Hemingway himself, who never disguised his admiration for those men who pitted themselves against real danger – especially soldiers, matadors, boxers and big-game hunters.

For a short time following his arrival back in the U.S., Hemingway was able to persuade others to view him in a similar light. Seizing an invaluable opportunity to begin creating the larger than life image he enthusiastically promoted of himself throughout his life, he was aided by the fact that he was both the first American to be wounded on the Italian front and the first to arrive home. Interviewed by the New York Sun Hemingway confirmed that he wanted to return to journalism and was looking for a newspaper "that wants a man that is not afraid of work and wounds." His arrival in New York had been reported in the Chicago American and the Kansas City Star and he would do full (and fulsome) interviews both with the former and Trapeze, the high school magazine he had once edited so distinctively.

Awarded $1,400 insurance benefits for his injuries, Hemingway took advantage of this windfall to take a year out, living mainly at home. In February he was guest of honor at a party thrown by members of Chicago's Italian community, gave a talk to Oak Park High School students in March (enlivened graphically by the brandishing of the blood-encrusted trousers he'd been wearing when injured, a gas mask and an Austrian service revolver) and undertook an eight-town lecture tour of clubs, churches and schools for the princely fee of $10 each.

Psychologically, however, Ernest Hemingway was a mess. He began to interpret his family's natural concern and solicitude as pity for a cripple, had a number of rows with his parents and was clearly troubled by the exaggerations he'd inserted into his versions of events in Italy – enough to use the musings of Harold Krebs, central character in his short story *Soldier's Home,* to help purge that guilt: "To be listened to at all he had to lie . . . His lies were quite unimportant lies and consisted in attributing to himself things other men had seen, done or heard of . . ."

Fishing trips to the northern tip of Michigan with old high school buddies, which would prove the inspiration for his story *Big Two-Hearted River,* revived in him an interest in both writing and romance. It was a 17-year-old freckled redhead called Marjorie Bump (sic) who served as catalyst for the latter. Although she was unconditionally attracted to the young war hero, surely enough for their relationship to have been a success, Marjorie was destined to serve only as inspiration for two Nick Adams stories – *The Three-Day Blow* and *The End of Something* – both of which cast a jaundiced eye back to the end of unsatisfactory love affairs.

Despite his drunken ramblings to Chink Dorman-Smith of week-long couplings with an insatiable Sicilian woman, it is generally accepted

that Ernest Hemingway finally lost his virginity in the summer of 1919, while staying with Oak Park friends of his family, Jim and Liz Dilworth, at their holiday home in Michigan. Several years older than him and a waitress in a local restaurant, the woman's initiation of Hemingway into carnal delights would make their way into print as *Up in Michigan,* one of the *Three Stories and Ten Poems* privately published in Paris by Bill Bird in 1923, but which Horace Liveright cautiously omitted from trade editions of the early collection *In Our Time.*

Hemingway's graphic description (". . . She was frightened but she wanted it. She had to have it but it frightened her . . .") of the sexual encounter was considered unprintable by Gertrude Stein and would appall his family, not least because he called his rutting couple Jim and Liz – their friends' real names, of course.

He would draw on real life, too, during the two months he spent lodging at Potter's Rooming House in Petoskey, a small town on Lake Michigan. Destined to become the setting for his satire *The Torrents of Spring,* it would also be the base from which he sent two short stories – *The Passing of Pickles McCarty,* or *The Woppian Way* and *Wolves and Doughnuts* – to the editors of the Popular Magazine and the Saturday Evening Post respectively. The former (with its awful pun on the Appian Way in its title) was the story of an Italian boxer fighting under an Irish alias who turns his back on a championship fight to join the Arditi and is unable to return to the relative tameness of boxing and a boring hometown once he's witnessed real action at the front. Crammed with Hemingway's own real and exaggerated war exploits, it was duly rejected, as was *Wolves and Doughnuts.*

His natural disappointment and sinking morale were to be shaken off by an unlikely savior at year-end. This was Harriet Connable, one of the audience who packed the Petoskey Public Library to hear what would be Hemingway's last war lecture. A friend of his mother's, Harriet was the wife of Ralph Connable, the man who had masterminded the rapid growth of the Woolworth empire in Canada – from an original ten stores in 1915 to more than 100 stores by 1919 – and the mother of Ralph, Jr., only a year younger than Hemingway and lame since infancy.

The Connables were planning to spend a month in Florida and were looking for a tutor–companion to stay with and draw out their amiable but shy and lonely son in the large graystone mansion they owned in Toronto. Ernest Hemingway, sportsman, war hero and aspiring writer, fitted the bill superbly. He was quick to accept their offer of $50 a month plus generous expenses (". . . to supply you," as Connable's letter explained, "with the necessary funds to pay for such entertainments and sports as you feel would lead [Ralph] along the right channel"), domestic servants at his beck and call and Ralph Sr.'s promise to introduce him to influential figures at the Toronto Star Weekly.

True to his word, Connable took Hemingway to meet – among others – the paper's Features Editor, Gregory Clark. Underwhelmed by his first impressions of what he would recall as a "large, rather heavy, loose-jointed youth" who appeared "shy, anxious and restless" and had "a queer, explosive way of describing things," Clark nevertheless fell under

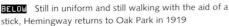
BELOW Still in uniform and still walking with the aid of a stick, Hemingway returns to Oak Park in 1919

ABOVE The Hemingway family, with Ernest far right, 1920

Hemingway's charm, accompanied him on fishing and skiing trips, and became a good friend to a man he characterized as "a weird combination of quivering sensitiveness and preoccupation with violence."

Thanks to Clark's recommendation and the weight of Ralph Connable's influence, Star Weekly editor J. Herbert Cranston (who didn't see Hemingway as "likely to develop into anything out of the ordinary") was prevailed upon to give him a chance to write some human interest features at a maximum possible fee of $10 per story. Writing up a storm, the tireless Hemingway submitted 11 stories which were published by the Star Weekly between February and mid-May, and another 22 stories between the end of his summer holiday at Walloon Lake and his departure for Europe, as a reporter for the Toronto Daily Star, in December 1921.

That was all very well and good, but Cranston's miserly fees meant that Hemingway would earn only $150 for his first year's work, and that fact would be only one of the long list of recriminations hurled at him by his mother during the summer when a misunderstanding led to an almighty row and his expulsion from Grace Cottage, the new holiday home his parents had built at Walloon Lake.

Ted Brumback was Hemingway's guest that summer – Ernest's 21st birthday – and it was just after they had celebrated the anniversary that Ursula, Sunny and two female friends decided to go out for a late night picnic without seeking parental permission. Hemingway and Brumback were dragooned into accompanying them. When they sneaked back, at 3 am, they were met by a fearsome sight – Grace Hemingway and the friends' mother, both of whom were convinced of and angered by the young men's lustful intentions.

All of Grace Hemingway's captious spite poured out during the next two days – Ernest was and had always been idle, a wanton parasite, irreligious, disrespectful and corrupt, and was now nothing but a wild pleasure-seeking loafer who traded on his looks to snare and corrupt young girls. She did not want him in "her" house, she told him forcefully in a note she'd hurriedly written, "until your tongue has learned not to insult and shame your mother." This from a woman who had already told her recuperating and emotionally frail son that he couldn't have had such a bad time of it in Italy since he'd spent most of it in hospital!

Worse was to follow. Alerted to the showdown by a letter from Grace, which included an allegation that Ernest had disparaged her choice of reading matter during a mid-row trading of insults, Ed Hemingway (who was back in Oak Park after having missed Ernest's coming-of-age celebrations) sided unconditionally with his wife and wrote confirming her demand that Ernest and Brumback stay away from Grace Cottage until they were "formally invited" to return.

It was unjust and unkind and must have been a severe embarrassment to be treated thus in front of a friend, but the episode served to help Hemingway begin shaking off the shackles in which Grace had kept him constrained for so long. The chasm which had suddenly, dramatically opened between them was never to be bridged, not even by uneasy truces, and while he would do right by Grace financially after Ed's

suicide (as he would the rest of his family), Hemingway's support was entirely driven by his sense of duty, and never by love. That was now irretrievably lost.

During October 1920 Hemingway moved into a large East Chicago Avenue apartment being rented by Kenley Smith (the advertising executive older brother of his long-time buddy, Bill, and widely known as "Y.K." – his first name being Yeremya) and Smith's wife, the pretty, petite but shiftless and feckless Genevieve, who boasted the glorious nickname of Doodles. In January 1921, when their short tenancy ended, the trio moved into a seven-room flat, with a cook, on East Division Street. In the meantime Hemingway, who was now eagerly soaking up Chicago's many diversions, including boxing tournaments, nights at the opera, dancing and tennis, had become a full-time journalist, albeit a poorly paid one ($40 a week at first, but raised to a less than princely $50 a week a month later) and then with a very odd publication.

Co-operative Commonwealth (The Magazine of Mutual Help) was published monthly by the Cooperative Society of America. Circulation was only 65,000, and it consisted of some 20 pages of advertisements and eight pages of editorial matter, most of which Hemingway created. This ranged from the human-interest features in which he now excelled to hastily-cobbled articles on such engrossing topics as the merits of some international co-operative enterprizes. One can only assume these were cobbled together from clippings and reports, for his knowledge of the world co-op movement was not known to be encyclopaedic.

The First Marriage – Hadley

It was through Y.K. and Doodles that Hemingway was to make two hugely important contacts – one professional, the other personal – which would combine to change the course of his life and career forever.

The first was Sherwood Anderson, the Ohio-born poet, short story writer and novelist who, with the likes of Carl Sandburg (whom Hemingway heard read at the Smiths' apartment), Theodore Dreiser, Ben Hecht and Edgar Lee Masters, had helped create a thriving Chicago literary movement. Anderson's prose style, which was largely based on everyday idiomatic speech, struck a major chord with Hemingway, who told the older man so. Flattered and reasonably impressed by sight of Hemingway's own early fictional efforts, Anderson (who had just returned from a six-month stay in Paris) urged Hemingway to do the same – he would never regret it.

When, in December 1921, Hemingway finally took his advice, Anderson generously supplied him with letters of introduction to Gertrude Stein, Ezra Pound and book publisher Sylvia Beach. It was a generosity Hemingway would repay in 1925 in the form of *Torrents of Spring,* a cruel parody of Anderson's distinctive style – a betrayal of a kindness which did Hemingway little credit.

It was in November 1920, shortly after he'd first moved in with Y.K. and Doodles Smith, that Hemingway first met Hadley Richardson.

Instantly entranced by her looks and vivacity, he is reputed to have told Smith: "That's the girl I'm going to marry!" the evening they were first introduced. A tall, strikingly attractive woman with red-gold hair and fabulous cheekbones – and eight years older than her future husband – Hadley brought her own formidable set of emotional baggage and psychological scars to a relationship which had the odds stacked against it from the word go by virtue of its protagonists' inexperience.

Born in St. Louis in November 1891, Hadley was the youngest of six children, only four of whom survived infancy. When she herself was tiny Hadley had fallen from a window, injured her back badly and was thereafter treated as an invalid by her mother, a devoted theosophist and dabbler in all things psychic. In 1903 her father, a pharmaceutical company director, shot himself in the midst of financial problems.

After accompanying her mother on a summer tour of Europe in 1909 she was enrolled at Bryn Mawr, the exclusive women's college (where, coincidentally, she'd been a classmate and close friend of Katy Smith, Bill and Y.K. Smith's sister), but dropped out after less than a year when she failed a course. In 1910 her sister died horribly when her clothes caught fire, while Hadley found herself caught up in a lesbian friendship with a married woman, Mrs. Rapallo, a flirtation she told Hemingway had never actually been consummated.

A gifted pianist who gave recitals in St. Louis, Hadley had also fallen in love with Harrison Williams, her teacher, who had rejected her. (Shades of Agnes and Ernest?) She had quit her musical career because she lacked the stamina (shades of Grace?), but after her mother died of nephritis – the same wasting disease that had claimed Grace Hemingway's father – in the autumn of 1920, she had been able to drop her invalid daughter role and do precisely what she wanted. Hadley was immeasurably aided in this by the $3,000-a-year trust fund that her mother had left her.

Hemingway's year-long courtship of the complex Hadley was unusual in many respects – not least because she was resident in St. Louis for most of its duration, so a great deal of it was carried out in the form of letters.

This appears to have only increased Hemingway's ardor, for his missives to his darling Hash (as Hadley had been nicknamed) were often very passionate. While always frank and open, Hadley's letters appeared more restrained, although they did openly discuss matters such as their own previous sexual experiences and opinions as well as topics like Havelock Ellis' descriptions and controversial theories of sexual behavior.

More than anything else, Hadley intended to reassure Hemingway that she fully reciprocated his feelings, and was prepared to submit herself almost entirely to his will and wishes in the future. It was a pledge she would keep throughout their marriage, even when it meant sterling displays of tolerance of his adultery when he was preparing to trade her in for a new and inevitably younger model.

ABOVE Hadley and Hemingway on their wedding day,
September 3, 1921

PREVIOUS PAGE The groom (center) on his wedding day
with his bachelor friends

The couple were married at the Horton Bay, Michigan, Methodist
church on September 3, 1921 – a choice brought about by its relative
proximity to the Hemingway family holiday home which Ed and Grace
had offered them for their honeymoon, hatchets having temporarily
been buried in an all-prevailing atmosphere of goodwill.

Hadley hadn't wanted to want to marry in her home town, where she
was convinced that her domineering older sister, Florence, would take
charge of arrangements. Strangely, given Hadley's past promises of complete submission, she acceded to Florence's pressure not to include the
word "obey" in her wedding vows.

Hemingway, who likened the last-minute wedding preparations to
those he'd witnessed in pre-fight dressing rooms and wondered if he
would feel the same way if he were bound for the scaffold, was ably
assisted through the ordeal by Bill Smith – his best man. Also on hand
to lend moral support were Ed and Grace, his sisters Ursula and Carol
(Marcelline was apparently prostrate with "her nerves" while Sunny was
away in Wisconsin, at a girls' camp), his kid brother Leicester and a
bunch of friends, including Carl Edgar, Katy Smith, Harriet Connable
and her son Ralph.

Y.K. and Doodles Smith were not there, however. During the summer Hemingway had fallen out with them. That much is certain,
although there are different versions as to how and why.

One has it that Hemingway discovered that Doodles was having an
affair, was appalled and offered to punch the interloper. He'd been dis-
suaded against this extreme course of action by Bill Smith, who also
made him promise not to tell Y.K. Hemingway, however, had blabbed
to a mutual friend who did spill the beans, and Hemingway was forced
to move out of their apartment.

The second version is that Doodles told Hemingway that Hadley had been flirting with "Dirty" Don Wright, the man with whom Doodles herself was mid-affair. Hadley denied it and when Hemingway learned that Wright had been the source of the gossip he threatened to dismember him. Whichever version is true, Y.K. and Doodles ceased to be Hemingway's friends.

He was also unemployed. Still writing occasional articles for the Toronto Weekly Star, he'd quit his full-time job at Co-operative Commonwealth in May, just before the entire U.S. Cooperative Society collapsed amid a slew of court actions for bankruptcy and fraud. But he had a pretty solid ace up his sleeve ready to play.

The newlyweds spent their two-week honeymoon fighting off bouts of influenza and food poisoning, during which Hemingway insisted on taking Hadley to Petoskey and introducing her to some of his old flames – including the gorgeously named Marjorie Bump. It was a bizarre episode and perhaps evidence of a still-prevailing insecurity on his part: Hadley had to be given first-hand proof that he was still missed by former girlfriends.

Their first home was a small, dismal flat on North Dearborn Street, but they put up with it in the knowledge that it was only going to be a short-term arrangement. The ace up Hemingway's sleeve was a long-standing offer of a job with the Toronto Daily Star, first made nine months earlier by its Editor, John Bone, who'd seen and liked Ernest's work for the Weekly Star. Already busy changing dollars for Italian lire (they planned to go to Rome), Hemingway called Bone and said he would work for the Star, but only if he was appointed its European correspondent. However, it was only after Bone agreed that Hemingway remembered Sherwood Anderson's advice and decided to make Paris, and not Rome, his base.

With Anderson's letters of introduction in his pocket and a new and even wealthier bride on his arm (Hadley's uncle Arthur had died in October, leaving her $8,000 better off), Ernest Hemingway set sail from New York on the French liner *Leopoldina* on December 8, 1921, his war heroism confirmed in the shape of the Medaglia d'Argento al Valore he had finally been given, with all due pomp, by General Armando Díaz at a Chicago banquet ceremony.

Ahead of him, the Old World waited to be explored and conquered.

BELOW The decorations awarded to Hemingway by the Italian government: left, the Croce di Guerra, and (right) the far more exclusive Medaglia d'Argento al Valore

the

grand tour

(1922-1924)

La Vie Parisienne:
Ezra Pound and Gertrude Stein

Paris was wreathed in damp winter air when Hemingway and Hadley arrived, heading for the relative warmth of l'Hôtel Jacob, which had the benefit of being not only cheap and clean but situated on the Left Bank, habitual haunt of painters, poets and other romantic rascals. Recommended to them by Sherwood Anderson, the hotel was also close to a number of café bars – two of which, the Dôme and the Rotonde, became firm Hemingway favorites – and restaurants, among which Le Pré aux Clercs was a godsend to newlyweds watching their pennies. Situated at the junction of rue Jacob and rue Bonaparte, its patron served a fair meal for two and a carafe of reasonable wine, for 12 francs, then about one dollar.

Their first social contact in Paris was Lewis Galantière, an exiled Chicagan friend of Sherwood Anderson's who worked as a translator and knew everyone who was anyone on the Parisian cultural scene. He and his girlfriend invited the Hemingways to be their guests for dinner at Michaud's, a regular eating place for the Irish writer James Joyce and what Hemingway called his "Celtic crew." The evening ended on a bizarre note when Hemingway, enlivened by good food, wines and liqueurs, challenged Galantière to a couple of rounds of sparring, during which he knocked off and broke his new friend's spectacles!

Despite this, it was Galantière who found the Hemingways their first French home, at 74 rue du Cardinal-Lemoine, an inexpensive apartment in an unprepossessing working-class district near Place de la Contrescarpe. Hemingway exaggerated its charms in letters home (the area boasted the 16th-century writer-priest François Rabelais as a former local) but would paint it in truer shabby shades in later recollections.

Wanting to escape the cold and damp of Paris and needing something by way of a feature to send back to the Toronto Star, Hemingway and Hadley decided to treat themselves to a second, more leisurely, honeymoon. Electing to go to Switzerland, they rented a chalet in Chamby-sur-Montreux, filled the place with lots of reading matter, piled the fireplace high with blazing logs and spent a truly romantic time immersed in each other's company. Hemingway's feature for the Star described some of the Swiss towns they passed through as not so much like anything he'd ever seen as "the deserted boomtowns of Nevada." Not that he'd ever been to Nevada, nor seen a deserted boomtown, but it was a great, evocative line.

Refreshed and invigorated, Hemingway got down to some serious writing once he and Hadley returned to Paris, renting a small room in a hotel as his workplace. True to form, Hemingway claimed it was the hotel in which the poet Verlaine had died in 1896. He didn't, but had ended his days in a lodging house run by Eugénie Krantz, a semi-retired prostitute. Perched atop the building at the end of many flights of precipitous stairs, Hemingway's eyrie boasted a wonderful view of the

LEFT The cathedral of the Sacred Heart – Sacré Coeur – dominates the Paris skyline from the top of Montmartre

PREVIOUS PAGE Hemingway, leaning forward to observe a crucial moment during a bullfight

city's rooftops and was the place where he began writing a whole slew of material – poems, stories, his early memories of Michigan, especially fishing trips with Bill Smith – in a growing pile of cheap notebooks.

This time, and the years that followed in Paris, were to prove the most creative, and truly productive, of his life. It was here that Hemingway found the spot within himself which marked him as special, gifted and unique. And if the words did not always flow easily, he was surrounded by people who understood the artistic process, could commiserate when writer's block struck, be trusted to give educated advice when asked, and knew how to celebrate properly when things came right. As it had done for countless generations of creative people in the past – and continues to do today – Paris worked its magic on Ernest Hemingway, liberated him, thrilled him and helped inspire him.

One of those who would emerge as a stalwart friend and influential contact was Gertrude Stein, the Pennsylvania-born writer, self-styled genius and eccentric whose Paris home was a magnet for most of the leading writers and artists who either lived in the city or were, like Hemingway, seeking some of its magic. It was also, as Hemingway and Hadley were to discover on their first visit to share tea and conversation with Stein and her companion, the equally eccentric Alice B. Toklas (and immediately nicknamed "Miss Tocraz" by the former Mr. Hemingstein), a palace filled with modern art treasures, collected by Gertrude and her brother, Leo, an accomplished art critic. These included the likes of Henri Matisse, Georges Braque, Paul Cézanne, Jean Renoir, Pierre Bonnard, Pablo Picasso (who painted Stein's portrait) and Juan Gris, hung side by side in what had become a temple devoted to the cream of the Post-Impressionist movement and new avant-garde Cubism.

Some 30 years later, when describing Stein's salon in the rue de Fleurus in his memoir *A Moveable Feast* (published posthumously in 1964), Hemingway wrote: "It was like one of the best rooms in the finest museum except there was a big fireplace and it was warm and comfortable and they gave you good things to eat and tea and natural distilled liqueurs made from purple plums, yellow plums or wild raspberries."

First impressions were mutually favorable. Hemingway liked the short, sturdy and big-breasted woman who, he said, had "beautiful eyes and a strong German-Jewish face," and reminded him of the peasant women he'd seen in northern Italy, mainly because of "her clothes, her mobile face and her lovely, thick, alive immigrant hair." He could listen to her chatter on for hours about people she'd met and places she'd been, and Gertrude Stein loved to chatter on for hours.

For her part, Stein instantly took to Hemingway, who she found extremely handsome and "rather foreign looking, with passionately interested, rather than interesting eyes." She had, of course, read none of Hemingway's creative work at this stage and was going only on Sherwood Anderson's recommendation that the newcomer was "an American writer instinctively in touch with everything worthwhile going on here." Writing to Anderson after the Hemingways had departed for their own, more humble accommodation, Stein informed him: "They are charming.

BELOW The old quarters of Paris were a magnet for the bohemian literati to which Hemingway was attracted

He is a delightful fellow and I like his talk. We have had a good time with them and hope to see more of them."

Hadley, by her own account, spent that first encounter in a funk, consigned, as all visitors' wives were, to a sideline seat with Alice B. Toklas. A tiny but pleasant woman, Alice managed to serve tea, do some needlepoint, and talk about various inconsequential subjects, while still joining in parts of the conversation Hemingway and Stein were having by the fireplace. Hadley was vaguely frightened by her, although better acquaintance would make her a good, valued and trusted friend.

Gertrude Stein's value to Hemingway was a debt he would acknowledge long after they had fallen out. It was his habit to meet her in the Luxembourg Gardens for long walks, during which he would soak up her theories of language and art, or call in at the house on rue du Fleurus where she could talk him through her collection of Cézannes, explaining how his methods had inspired her own unique writing style, which used repetition and subtle shifts in emphasis just as the painter used his brush to create light and shade.

It was a lesson well learned, for Hemingway would repeat Stein's theories of the wordsmith as painter, with especial reference and deference to Cézanne, in many of his future works. And it was thanks to Stein that the distinctive Hemingway "voice" first came into being, after she had finally read some of his early works. His poems were to her liking – they were, she said, "direct, Kiplingesque" – but the prose was overburdened with descriptions. Her instructions were simple, clear and invaluable: "Begin over and concentrate."

Paying tribute to Stein years later, Hemingway conceded that she had "discovered many truths about rhythms and the uses of words in repetition that were valid and valuable," or as he wrote to Bill Smith at the time, ". . . she's trying to get at the mechanics of language. Take it apart and see what makes it go." Sadly, communication with Smith ended soon after as Hemingway's childhood companion came off the fence and sided with Y.K. and Doodles in the still-festering row which had forced Hemingway from the apartment on East Division Street.

BELOW Montmartre in the '20s: there was the opportunity for much socializing in bars and cafes until the small hours

Hemingway would also readily own to the help he received from Ezra Pound during his early years in Paris, telling the poet himself that he had taught him "more about how to write and how not to write than any son of a bitch alive." That education included a stricture to mistrust adjectives, although Pound's tendency to pack his work with arcane references and facts led Hemingway to muse that he appeared incapable of leaving "any erudition true or false out of a poem." The Hemingway rule was that while a writer should know as much as he needed to write with authority, he should never actually use it.

The Hemingways first met Pound and his wife, Dorothy Shakespear, soon after their initial invitation to tea with Stein and "Miss Tocraz." The Pound household, an apartment at 70 bis Notre Dame des Champs, was a chilly clutter of papers, paintings, (by Dorothy and the English champion of Vorticism, Cecil Wyndham Lewis) oriental prints, some boxwood furniture hand-built by Pound, and was in stark contrast to the opulence of Gertrude Stein's residence. Although disconcerted by Pound's bohemian appearance, Hemingway sat in rapt attention, his attitude deferential, much to Hadley's surprise.

Being only 14 years older than Hemingway, Ezra Pound was too young to be a father-figure to match Gertrude Stein's imminent adoption as a surrogate mother. Pound had long since thrown off any traces of his small-town middle-class Presbyterian raising – initially in his home state of Idaho and thereafter in Pennsylvania – through his education at a military academy and at the University of Pennsylvania, where his studies and post-graduate work left him with a working knowledge of Latin, Greek, German, Italian, Spanish, Provençal and early Anglo-Saxon, as well as the beginnings of a life-long friendship with fellow poet William Carlos Williams.

BELOW Gertrude Stein (left) and her secretary Alice B. Toklas, in a photograph taken in New York in October 1934

Since 1908, when he quit his post of Professor of Romance Languages at Wabash Presbyterian College, in Indiana, Pound had lived a gypsy life which had taken in Spain, Venice (the city in which he would die, in 1972) and London, where he achieved his first great successes with two volumes of poetry, *Personae* and *Exultations.* After an abortive return home in a vain attempt to make a literary living, he spent most of 1911 travelling in Italy, Germany and France before returning to London and a nine-year sinecure post as contributor to New Age, a socialist weekly.

In 1912 Pound had become London correspondent of the small Chicago-based magazine, Poetry; was one of the first to review and champion D.H. Lawrence, Robert Frost and sculptor Jacob Epstein; had begun a collaboration with the then-unknown James Joyce (the publication of whose *Portrait of the Artist as a Young Man* he helped arrange); and continued his rise to prominence as a poet in his own right. A friend of W.B. Yeats and T.S. Eliot, Pound had most notably led the way in using direct, sparse language and images to capture the poetic essence of experiences in writing.

Even as he and Dorothy entertained Hemingway and Hadley at tea, Pound was working on editing Eliot's masterpiece *The Waste Land* and acting as Paris correspondent for The Dial, the New York literary journal. A man of influence, then, besides being an influential poet, it would do Hemingway no harm to cultivate Ezra Pound both as an important contact and a potential opener of important doors.

While Pound did pitch some of Hemingway's poems to Scofield Thayer at The Dial ("I think, as you know, that the Dial shd occasionally take in a little new blood, and H seems to me as sound a chance as is likely to offer," Pound wrote in his covering letter), Thayer found the idea of publishing Hemingway completely resistible. Telling Pound that he thought The Dial already had "enough young blood . . . to make it decidedly rough reading," he also began the process of firing him, so getting rid of a man who, within eight years, would publish the first segments of *Cantos,* the ambitious epic he had begun in 1915 and would spend the rest of his life revising and completing.

Hemingway and Pound shared many poetic-literary ideals – a love of using profanities to scandalize ladies and terrify publishers, and an interest in boxing (Wyndham Lewis witnessed one of their sessions, which climaxed with a frustrated Pound collapsing into a chair, while Hemingway told Sherwood Anderson that his pupil had "the general grace of a crayfish" and a terrible tendency to lead with his chin). But they differed hugely, and noisily, when it came to politics and economics.

Suffice it to say that Pound was a committed socialist who subscribed to the conspiracy theories propounded by the Social Credit Movement that avaricious banks and international Jewry were responsible for everything that ailed the world. When Hemingway's star began ascending, Pound claimed that he had "sold himself to the god dollar."

There was never to be any falling out between Hemingway and Sylvia Beach, the last member of the holy trinity to whom Sherwood Anderson had directed and commended his young protégé. From the moment they met at her renowned bookstore, Shakespeare and Company, Sylvia Beach

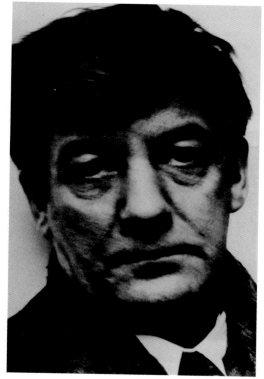

BELOW Sherwood Anderson, photo by Alfred Stieglitz

would be Hemingway's champion and fully deserving of his statement: "No one that I ever knew was nicer to me."

Even without Anderson's introduction Hemingway would have made his way to Beach's unique emporium on the rue de l'Odéon, a veritable treasure trove of literature old and new, classical and modern, including English, European and American poetry and art journals, much of which – if purchasing was an economic impossibility to a customer – could be borrowed, for a few centimes, from the lending library section. Inevitably, it was this facility which the young newcomer used most in the beginning, giving him access to an even wider world of words.

A Presbyterian minister's daughter, Sylvia Beach ("Brown eyes that were alive as a small animal's and as gay as a young girl's") lived in quiet harmony with her life companion, Adrienne Monnier, in the latter's apartment, not far from Shakespeare and Company. Nearer than that – just across the rue de l'Odéon, in fact – was Monnier's own bookstore, La Maison des Amis des Livres, itself the haunt of such book-lovers as Apollinaire (who once affected hurt that his newest collection, *Alcools,* was not in stock), Jean Cocteau, Erik Satie and André Gide, who would be forced to defend himself against Monnier's observation that his *Les Faux-Monnayeurs* (*The Counterfeiters*) showed that he was fundamentally cold and unkind.

Shakespeare and Company, in turn, was the chosen retreat for English-speaking novelists, artists, poets and Anglophile Sorbonne University students. Man Ray was the store's "official" photographer. Ezra Pound had a favorite chair near the big stove which heated the ground floor area, while James Joyce hovered incessantly, his thoughts doubtless rapt in the prospect of the imminent publication by Sylvia Beach of his new novel, *Ulysses.* This was achieved by persuading customers, friends and patrons to subscribe to the first edition – something Hemingway did with alacrity, pride and pleasure.

Another Shakespeare and Company regular was Robert McAlmon, the bisexual publisher of the Contact Editions of contemporary authors, who used Beach's premises as his business postal address and storage facility for unsold stock. It would be McAlmon who published Hemingway's first book, *Three Stories and Ten Poems,* in November 1923, while it was Adrienne Monnier who published the first French translation of a Hemingway story *L'Invincible* (The Undefeated) in her magazine, Le Navire d'argent.

Sylvia Beach and Monnier took to Hemingway and Hadley at once and it was only a matter of time before he returned their hospitality by introducing them to the previously unknown (to them) joys of six-day cycling marathons and, inevitably, boxing. It was all a world away from their milieu which was devoted exclusively to things sensitive and artistic.

Their acceptance of, and friendship with, Hemingway was also a break from self-imposed tradition – most of their male acquaintances were homosexual, which Hemingway was belligerently not. If anything, he was virulently homophobic (as he would prove countless times in print with unsympathetic portrayals of gay male characters). Strangely, perhaps, Hemingway harbored a fascination with lesbian relationships

BELOW Ezra Pound in the garden of his Paris studio, 1923

BOTTOM A Toronto Star Weekly piece from October 1923, in which Hemingway appeared to condemn bullfighting but at the same time romanticize it

(again, a subject to which he returned many times through the years), which is some explanation for his easy acceptance of the arrangements which Gertrude Stein and Alice Toklas, Sylvia Beach and Adrienne Monnier had made for themselves.

He was also fascinated by the whirligig social life of fellow expatriates, using the Toronto Star to paint a series of unflattering (though undoubtedly titillating to his provincial Canadian readers) features about the giddy, selfish hedonists who populated such Paris nightspots as La Coupole, Le Dôme, Boeuf sur le Troit, Les Deux Magots, La Rotonde and Dingo, Hemingway's retreat of choice, where Jimmie Charters, the voluble cockney barman, held court.

He was never short of fresh material as the likes of millionaire heiresses Peggy Guggenheim and Nancy Cunard rubbed shoulders (and more) with those of Harry Crosby, the playboy nephew of billionaire J.P. Morgan; surrealists André Breton, René Crevel and Louis Aragon; innumerable Russian émigrés (all claiming royal titles); poet e.e. cummings and English painter Nina Hamnett – among a cast of thousands more, all of whom were determined to have a fine old time of it. "Paris," he pronounced grandly, "is the Mecca of the bluffers and fakers in every line of endeavor from music to prizefighting."

Secure in the knowledge that none of these, or their friends, were likely to subscribe to the Star, Hemingway was free with his criticism of the goings-on around him, especially the more outrageous, bohemian figures ("a strange-acting and strange-looking breed," he also characterized as "the scum of Greenwich Village"), many of whom were his supposed friends. Hemingway was never going to be a bohemian, acquiring an exquisitely tailored Irish tweed suit soon after arriving in Paris to ensure that he always cut a fine figure as he strolled along the boulevards or sat, notebook and pen at the ready, taking a working break in some café.

Whenever possible, Hemingway and Hadley (who was quickly learning how to drink until dawn) would repair to local bars where the real Parisians – hoodlums, whores, sailors and the ubiquitous apaches – could be found dancing and making out to the accompaniment of accordions and guitars.

While he bemoaned the amount of time the Star stole from his schedule (when he'd much rather have been doing "real" writing), Hemingway had a golden rule never to miss the Wednesday meetings at the Anglo-American Press Club. An invaluable source of gossip and news about the world outside, it boasted such hard newsmen as Frank Mason of the Hearst-owned International News Service, and Guy Hickock of the Brooklyn Daily Eagle.

It would be in Hickock's old car that he and Hemingway would drive through Mussolini's brave new Italy and pen a biting sketch for The New Republic, Hickock who would supply him with press tickets and passes for sports events, and Hickock who would add to the Hemingway legend by reporting his war adventures to Eagle readers. For his part, Frank Mason added to the Hemingway coffers by hiring him as a back-up on tricky assignments.

Conferences and Corridas

Hemingway's real baptism of fire as a working journalist came in March 1922, when Toronto Star editor John Bone asked him to cover the International Economic Conference which was due to take place in Genoa, Italy. The 22-year old's return to Italy was to be as witness to the first major diplomatic forum since the Versailles conference which had redrawn many of the world's boundaries at the end of the 1914–18 war. It was a heavy responsibility for Hemingway, which he was to meet with distinction.

An eager, quick and clever student, Hemingway was also smart enough to know when to shut up and listen and when to raise one's head above the parapets. He also had the natural bravado of youth, which meant that he was able to secure interviews with many of the leading players, including British Prime Minister David Lloyd George ("the greatest compromizer politics has ever seen," he wrote of the Welsh Wizard's negotiating skills and, more personally: "the complexion of a boy subaltern just out of Sandhurst"); Soviet Foreign Minister Georgi Chicherin (four years earlier a political detainee in one of Britain's prisons); and his deputy, Maxim Litvinov (wartime Bolshevik ambassador to the Court of St. James, but expelled by Lloyd George).

Dispatching 23 stories to the Star between April 10 and May 13, Hemingway packed his letters and cables with wonderful detail, not only of key delegates – Germany's Foreign Minister, Walter Rathenau, boasted a "polished billiard-ball head," while his Chancellor, Joseph Wirth, looked like "a tuba player in a German band" – but also of the sights which greeted him in Genoa's streets.

Armed police patrolled everywhere, ready to separate the gangs of Communists and up-and-coming *fascisti* who would attack each other at will. He was disparaging of both: the Communists were "good fathers and good workingmen who drank in the cafés . . . and chalked up slogans on their way home," while the Fascists posed "almost as great a danger to the peace of Italy."

Much of Hemingway's prescience, especially when it came to dissecting and explaining the often complex political implications of machinations inside the conference hall, came from the "shut up and listen" school of journalism. Wisely, he picked up most of his hard information from the more seasoned men around him, like Max Eastman, the American editor-journalist who was covering the conference for the New York World while en route for Russia, London Daily Herald reporter George Slocombe, and Chicago Tribune Central European Bureau chief George Seldes. Acquaintance with Max Eastman led to a friendship which would be resumed in Paris, although Eastman's attempts to place some of Hemingway's jottings ("They weren't stories," said Eastman, "They were just a paragraph or two long") with his old paper, The Liberator, came to nothing.

Back in Paris, Hemingway learned that the May issue of The Double-Dealer, a New Orleans magazine that included Sherwood Anderson and

ABOVE The bustling Rue de Rivoli in Paris between the wars

the young critic, Edmund Wilson, among its regular contributors, featured *A Divine Gesture,* a comic fable about a hassled God and archangel Gabriel in the Garden of Eden which he'd written before leaving Chicago and had left with Anderson, who had persuaded The Double-Dealer to publish it.

A month later the magazine ran Hemingway's wry quatrain, *Ultimately:* "He tried to spit out the truth;/Dry mouthed at first/He drooled and slobbered in the end;/Truth dribbling his chin." Sharing the page was *Portrait,* a poem by William Faulkner, another Nobel laureate-in-waiting whom Sherwood Anderson would also generously help to find the first rung of the publishing ladder.

It was time for a vacation, and for Hadley to meet Chink Dorman-Smith, Hemingway's wartime friend. Returning to Chamby-sur-Montreux, they planned fishing and mountain-climbing before Hadley was taken on a pilgrimage to the scenes of his Red Cross heroism.

Their plans were delayed by the possibility that Hemingway may be allowed to go to Russia for the Star, but that came to nothing (despite Litvinov's assurances in Genoa that an entry visa was no problem) as Soviet red tape and snail-paced bureaucracy conspired to end the dream. One can only imagine what Hemingway, no socialist and certainly no lover of totalitarian regimes, would have made of Lenin's earthly nirvana.

By mid-May the trio were immersed in their vacation, Hemingway writing glowing notes to his father about the Swiss wildlife and fishing. Hadley was, he said, "as red and brown as an Indian," although she suffered for her vanity in wearing unsuitable shoes on a gruelling hike they took through the St. Bernard Pass, still covered with thick snow. Travelling by train to Milan, from where Dorman-Smith returned to his regiment in Cologne, Hemingway informed Gertrude Stein that Hadley was employing "alcoholic clairvoyance" to pick race winners at San Siro, the scene of previous happy outings with Agnes Von Kurowsky.

Before leaving Milan, Hemingway was granted his first interview with Benito Mussolini, still five months away from ordering his Fascist blackshirts to march on Rome but still revelling in the success of their recent attack on Bologna, where opponents had been beaten up and offices fire-bombed. Although he would denounce il Duce as a bullying fraud within a year, Hemingway was initially impressed by the big, tanned man who spent the interview, held in the offices of Il Popolo d'Italia newspaper, fondling a wolfhound puppy's ears.

A clever propagandist (as befitted a one-time journalist and newspaper editor), Mussolini was able to sell Hemingway the carefully manicured version of his role in W.W. I, which included his early volunteering for duty, decorations for bravery and serious wounds inflicted while fighting with the élite Bersagliere Corps. The truth – his enlistment was the result of enforced conscription in October 1915, five months after Italy declared war on Austria, while his injuries were caused by an accident during a training exercise in 1917 – would remain buried despite the best efforts of his opponents and contribute to the early conversion to him and sympathy for the Fascist cause from Winston Churchill, the campaigning American writer Lincoln Steffens, conductor Arturo

Toscanini, Irish playwright George Bernard Shaw and Ezra Pound, among many other influential figures.

The fact that Hemingway managed to get a few key facts in his first article wrong – including Mussolini's age (he was then 39 years old) and birthplace – suggest an over-ready willingness to trust the "official" Fascist biography. Mussolini, he advised Canadians, was "not the monster he has been pictured" but a patriot fighting a brave war against encroaching Communism who liked nothing more than watching Laurel and Hardy comedies in his private projection suite.

Going back to "his" war was a mistake, Hemingway quickly realized and it was an unhappy fact he readily shared with his Toronto Star readers. In Schio his old barracks was now a factory, while the town of Fossalta di Piave had been rebuilt in ugly utilitarian fashion. There was no sign of the trenches. As for the river, once muddy and bloodied, it was now clear and blue, its only activity a team of horses hauling a cement barge. Warning his fellow veterans against considering a return, Hemingway mourned that the past was ". . . as dead as a busted Victrola record. Chasing yesterdays is a bum show." This was fine advice from a man who was to spend so much time chasing, and so creatively recreating, his own yesterdays.

Back to a slow summer in Paris, Hemingway filed a number of desultory sketches for the Star, but persuaded William Bird, U.S. journalist and aspiring publisher, to appoint Ezra Pound editor for a series of new limited-run private editions for Bird's infant Three Mountains Press. Flattered, Pound agreed, settling on new works by Williams Carlos Williams, himself, T.S. Eliot, Ford Madox Ford, Cecil Wyndham Lewis . . . and Hemingway. In time, Bill Bird would be the man who published *A Draft of XVI Cantos of Ezra Pound,* although the batch Hemingway discussed with him eventually included Williams' *The Great American Novel* and, in 1924, Ernest Hemingway's *In Our Time.*

A two-week hiking holiday in the Black Forest – for which Hemingway and Hadley were accompanied by Lewis Galantière and his fiancée, Dorothy Butler, Bill and Sally Bird – was not a success in social terms. None of them liked Dorothy Butler who later received a splenetic hurtful letter from Hemingway telling her she was "a selfish bitch" he had only endured for Galantière's sake.

The collapse of Germany's post-war economy ("Because the mark keeps dropping we have more money than when we started two weeks ago," he told his family) led to widespread riots, one of which he and Hadley witnessed in Cologne while visiting Chink Dorman-Smith, and Hemingway translated into a powerful feature for the Toronto Star Weekly describing the drowning of a policeman who tried to stop rioters. Chink was the source of a chilling detail Hemingway used as color: as French troops finally pulled out of occupied Silesia, local girls who'd fraternized with them were being ritually stripped, shaved and driven from their homes. A wound was festering, ready to be picked at within a few years by Adolf Hitler.

Thanks to Bill Bird, in September Hemingway was granted a share in an audience with Georges Clemenceau, the 81-year old former French

OPPOSITE, TOP Ezra Pound

OPPOSITE, BOTTOM Constant companions Alice B Toklas and Gertrude Stein in an open car.

premier, who was about to undertake a lecture tour of the United States. Clemenceau's disinterest in visiting Canada (wrongly stating that the Canadians had "rejected compulsory military service to help out France" during the war) was enough for Hemingway's story to be "spiked" by John Bone, a rejection which rankled with Hemingway for many years.

Bone had not lost faith in his Paris correspondent, however, for in late September Hemingway embarked on a long, dangerous and arduous journey which would take him via Greece, Serbia and Bulgaria (a country he had written about previously, despite never having been there) to Constantinople, capital of a Turkey that was still under Allied protection but riven by the last stages of a brutal Greco-Turkish war. With the Turkish army of Mustapha Kemal moving inexorably towards Constantinople, it was a showdown Hemingway wanted to witness first-hand, even if his wife was violently opposed to his going and refused to speak to him for three days before departure.

Hemingway spent three weeks on this mission, living in a succession of flea-ridden hotels and filing reports for both the Star and the International News Service – a secret deal with Frank Mason which led John Bone to complain that many of his dispatches bore a disturbing similarity to INS bulletins! Military censors did their best to ensure that some of Hemingway's cables did not get sent until they were old news, and none of them evaded their blue pencils.

As ever, he was quick to make contact with seasoned war-watchers – in this case Charles Sweeney, a mercenary who advised Hemingway on military strategy, and two British officers, Major Johnson and Captain Wittal, who were press liaison men in Constantinople. Both had observed the Greek defeat in Anatolia a few weeks earlier, including the massacre of Greek infantry by their own artillery – what modern military men now euphemistically call "friendly fire." Hemingway would not only draw on Wittal's account of that débâcle for the Star but hoard it for 15 years and use in *The Snows of Kilimanjaro* as part of the dying Harry Walden's memories: ". . . and the artillery had fired into the troops and the British observer had cried like a child."

Watching the real cost of war near Thrace: the miles of bewildered frightened dispossessed trudging through rain and mud in a vain attempt to escape the fighting; the mindless brutality of soldiers from both sides who were as scared as the civilians; the filth, poverty and disease; and the whores and hustlers for whom war was just another business opportunity, proved too much to stomach and, in a way, determined Hemingway to cease being a journalist as soon as he could. It did not, however, prevent him filing a powerful account of the sights he'd witnessed.

Back in Paris by October 21, lice-ridden and exhausted, he and Hadley made up and made love – but only after he'd bathed and been de-bugged, one assumes. A month later, when he would normally have been one of those watching some of France's most famous politicians, writers, artists and Académie Française illuminati at the funeral of Marcel Proust, at the church of St-Pierre-de-Chaillot, Hemingway was on a train to Switzerland and the Lausanne Conference called to settle territorial disputes outstanding from the Greco-Turkish War.

Having arranged yet another under-the-table deal to cover the conference for both INS and the Universal News Service, another Hearst organization, while officially representing The Toronto Star, Hemingway was soon complaining to Hadley via letters and cables – she had succumbed to a bad cold but planned to join him in Chamby once the conference had finished – that his schedule was intolerable. Worse still, Frank Mason wasn't paying him enough for taxis to be affordable so Hemingway was haring from one delegation's hotel HQ to another, either on foot or by electric tram.

Prior to his departure Hemingway had met Ford Madox Ford at Ezra Pound's studio. It was not a meeting of minds, but Ford was a man of influence so one of Hemingway's priorities was to ensure that Hadley maintained contact with him. Ford, who had founded The English Review in 1908 and was the first to publish D.H. Lawrence, was in Paris for a month before taking his wife to St-Jean-Cap-Ferrat. The man may have been, as Hemingway maintained, a complete fraud, but he was a well-connected, well-considered and, above all, influential fraud.

Of greater influence, however, was Benito Mussolini who, since he'd given Hemingway his interview in Milan five months earlier, had become dictator of Italy. His blackshirts had marched into Rome to stage the seizure of power their leader deemed necessary to stamp his authority over a government which had already submitted to his demands. Watching Mussolini in full arrogant flow, arriving late for the inaugural conference session, strutting the world stage, Hemingway did a complete about-turn, describing him as "the biggest bluff in Europe" who had a "genius for clothing small ideas in big words." There is no proof that this led, as Hemingway claimed, to Mussolini issuing an edict barring him from setting foot in Italy again.

It was at Lausanne that Hemingway met the young South African-born journalist William Bolitho Ryall, a man he would credit as giving him ". . . the beginning of whatever education I received in international politics" during the evenings they spent talking and depleting their hotel's brandy stock with gusto. A noted caustic wit, Ryall – who represented the Manchester Guardian – had a reputation for pricking the pomposity of political leaders, a practice that Hemingway was all too ready to adopt in a series of Star features which pointedly turned against some of those he had so recently praised.

Most notable among these was Georgi Chicherin, who was once depicted by Hemingway as a brilliant, tireless diplomat, but was now mocked for wearing military-style uniforms and – horror of horrors – subject of a rumor that he had been dressed as a girl into late childhood. Hemingway's put-down ("The boy who was kept in dresses until he was twelve years old always wanted to be a soldier. And soldiers make empires and empires make wars") was not merely what biographer James R. Mellow has called "a glib psychological conclusion," but an uncomfortable echo of Hemingway's own enforced endurance of similar feminization by his mother.

Hemingway's disillusionment with the sheer hard slog of journalism had already been encouraged by Gertrude Stein: "If you keep on doing

ABOVE A typical bullfight in 1922

newspaper work you will never see things, you will only see words and that will not do, that is of course if you intend to be a writer," she'd told him. Stein's advice would be reinforced by Ryall, who had encouraged a number of young journalists to leave the trade before they burned out with their creative juices drained.

Further weight was provided by Lincoln Steffens, still a Mussolini supporter, who complimented Hemingway on his vivid report on the Greek retreat from Thrace. Emboldened by Steffens' comments, Hemingway gave him a copy of *My Old Man,* a short story he'd recently completed and taken to Lausanne. Impressed by Hemingway's tale of a young American boy's growing awareness that his beloved father, a jockey, is involved in race fixing, and climaxing with the father's death and the son's condemnation of a world which has exposed his chicanery, Steffens agreed to send it to Ray Long, editor of Cosmopolitan magazine.

It was fortuitous that Steffens kept his word, for disaster was about to strike the ambitious young Hemingway. It came as Hadley was leaving Paris for Switzerland, where she, Hemingway and Chink Dorman-Smith were to spend the Christmas–New Year holidays at Chamby. Among her luggage was a valise containing all she could find of Hemingway's recent stories and poems. This vanished at the Gare de Lyon and, despite a fevered and tearful hunt before her train pulled out, Hadley arrived in Lausanne on December 3 without this precious piece of cargo. Hemingway's alarm was modified by the thought that Hadley had surely not included the carbon copies of his last year's efforts. He was wrong.

Hemingway's version of the story was that he raced to Paris, hunted in vain for the carbons and was consoled by Stein and Toklas. This was not true – the flat and the Gare de Lyon's lost property offices were later searched by Guy Hickock and Lincoln Steffens. And, while Stein and "Miss Tocraz" were doubtless sympathetic and supportive, they expressed their regret from Provence where they stayed until February 1923. Through Bill Bird, some reward advertisements were published for the safe return of the valise and its contents, but with no response. Steffens wrote regretfully: "I am sorry, but I guess you will have to re-write your 'early works' or do better things hereafter to make up for them."

Hemingway did not return to Paris until he had completed his holiday in Chamby, enjoying "the kind of Christmas you can only get on top of the world," he wrote later. Not the action of a man prostrate with grief at losing all his literary works – which he hadn't. There was, for example, a trunk full of stories, poems and notes in Oak Park, most of which would eventually resurface. If Hemingway had lost the manuscript of his first novel, he would have been distraught. He was not, and he embarked on a carefree week of skiing and sledding with Chink and Hadley, the villain of the episode, suggesting that he had probably lost some working notes, perhaps with a few passages completed.

He dismissively described the lost treasures as his "Juvenilia" to Pound, who replied that Hemingway should view it as an "act of Gawd" and start work rewriting from memory, advising him to remember that "If the thing wobbles and won't reform, then it had no proper construction & never wd have been right . . ." Stein too gave him similar advice.

Inevitably, Hemingway stored the episode for future use, not only repeating his version of events in *A Moveable Feast,* but dramatizing the scenario in *The Garden of Eden.* In that, writer David Bourne is horrified when his wife, Catherine, deliberately burns all his notebooks and manuscripts, feeling no guilt because her financial support of him gave her, she believed, claim of ownership. As Hadley's trust fund helped them live better than Hemingway's earnings from journalism would have allowed, this may have been his expression of a long-held resentment. It is also possible that aspects of Zelda Fitzgerald's later jealousy of her husband's work contributed to the portrayal of Catherine Bourne.

Fatherhood and Flickers of Fame

In February 1923 the Hemingways travelled to Italy for a short walking tour of the Romagna region with Ezra and Dorothy Pound, basing themselves in the coastal town of Rapallo, near Genoa, where Pound was researching and beginning work on the cantos inspired by Sigismondo Malatesta, the Renaissance arts patron and political power broker. It was shortly after he returned from Italy that Hemingway visited Gertrude Stein to inform her that Hadley was pregnant.

According to Stein, who would include her own amusing account of that day in *The Autobiography of Alice B. Toklas,* Hemingway's announcement was made "with great bitterness." He was, he told her, "too young to be a father." Hemingway's reading of the same episode, made in a letter to Ezra Pound when Stein's version was published, was

GREGORY PECK in **Schnee am**
KILIMANDSCHARO
SUSAN HAYWARD·AVA GARDNER·HILDEGARD KNEF

ABOVE Although the majority of the narrative was set in Africa, in *The Snows of Kilimanjaro* – as in these stills from the 1950s film – the flashbacks included semi-autobiographical accounts of wartime action and bullfights

that he had simply been expressing doubts because he didn't have enough money to support a family and concentrate on his creative writing. However, other friends – including Guy Hickock – had clear memories of Hemingway's serious reservations and dismay at impending fatherhood, a fact that was borne out by Hemingway's continued suggestions to John Bone of story assignments which would take him away from Paris for long periods of time.

In March Hemingway repaid Gertrude Stein's kindnesses by writing a review of her *Geography and Plays,* a collection he praised highly, as he did its author ("Gertrude Stein is probably the most first rate intelligence employed in writing today") while getting in a few digs at the literary establishment and other writers he obviously considered over-rated, including Sinclair Lewis, H.L. Mencken, D.H. Lawrence and H.G. Wells. He also damned Sherwood Anderson's introduction to *Geography and Plays* with faint praise, so marking the first overt example of his decision to cut loose from Anderson's patronage and style.

While in Rapallo Hemingway had become re-acquainted with Henry "Mike" Strater, a Princeton painter friend of Scott Fitzgerald, who'd used the tall and excitable artist (who stammered when anxious) as the model for the pacifist-philosopher Burne Holiday in his 1920 novel *This Side of Paradise.* Plans for Hemingway and Mike Strater to indulge in some boxing were scotched when Strater sprained an ankle, but he used his incapacity to paint a new portrait of Hemingway – he'd already completed one, earlier, in Auteuil – and one of Hadley which Hemingway described to Stein as "corking."

It was also in Rapallo that he first met Edward J O'Brien, editor of the *Best Short Stories* collections published annually by the Boston firm Small, Maynard and Company. When shown a copy of *My Old Man,* O'Brien was impressed enough to announce that he would include it in his 1923 volume, despite the fact that it had not yet appeared in print. More, he would dedicate the entire collection to the vibrant newcomer although he would, unfortunately, give his name as "Hemenway."

Given that the expatriate artist colony in Paris was so compact and incestuous, it's surprising that Hemingway and Robert McAlmon's paths had not crossed until Rapallo, where the latter stopped over. He was on his way from Venice to the French Riviera, and spent time with his fellow Americans. He soon took to Hemingway, they exchanged copies of each other's works and McAlmon decided to publish a Hemingway collection through his own Contact Editions.

So it was, in the late summer of 1923, that Ernest Hemingway finally made it between hard covers, albeit in a very slim volume entitled *Three Stories and Ten Poems.* The stories McAlmon selected were *My Old Man, Out of Season* and *Up In Michigan* (possibly selected by McAlmon simply because of its potential for sales-boosting controversy). The poems consisted of six that Harriet Monroe had already published in Poetry magazine, plus two written in Chicago (*Oklahoma* and *Captive*s) and two that were composed in Paris, *Montparnasse* and *Along With Youth.*

Although McAlmon had stolen a march on Bill Bird's plans to publish *In Our Time* as Hemingway's début, Bird kept faith with

Hemingway even though he had to revise the contents of his volume hurriedly, having planned on using some of the material McAlmon had already selected.

Meanwhile, the Spring 1923 "Exiles" edition of *The Little Review*, published by Jane Heap and Margaret Anderson, featured six Hemingway vignettes which were arguably the most accomplished, sharpest, incisive and important products of the previous winter. Only one of these impressionistic word-pictures (a re-working of one of his Star reports from Greece) was based on his own experiences. Among the others were one told in a British officer-class British "voice" and was probably based on one of Chink Dorman-Smith's war tales. Another, describing the execution of six Greek politicians in Constantinople, was inspired by contemporary newspaper accounts, while a beautifully observed description of a bullfight owed a debt of gratitude to graphic accounts given him by Mike Strater, Gertrude Stein and Alice Toklas – Hemingway had yet to witness a corrida himself.

That ambition would finally be realized at the end of May when McAlmon invited Hemingway to Madrid and follow a bullfighting trail which would end in Granada, taking in Seville and Ronda along the way. Bill Bird would join them in Madrid, by which time Hemingway was an enthusiastic convert to the sport, its major stars, and to the fearsome creatures with whom the human participants did battle.

The trip was not an undiluted success. McAlmon was surprisingly squeamish when confronted with the bloodier and harsher realities of the bullring. He was also a prodigious drinker and Hemingway complained to Bird that McAlmon's insistence at partying every night was stealing time that he would have preferred to spend at work. Nevertheless, and extensive bar-hopping notwithstanding, Hemingway was filling notebooks with flashes of observed detail which would emerge initially as some of the vignettes in Bill Bird's *In Our Time* and later as potent background color for both *The Sun Also Rises* and *Death in the Afternoon* – his most public statements of the love he had for bullfighting.

Dissecting it for Toronto Star readers, Hemingway would describe the corrida as "less a sport than a tragedy," telling them: "The tragedy is the death of the bull, the inevitable death of the bull – the terrible, almost prehistoric bull." His admiration for the matadors knew no bounds, his especial reverence being reserved for the chubby-faced Chicuelo, a Madrid favorite, and the fast-rising Nicanor Villalta who, he said, stalked the arena "like a young wolf."

It was at Gertrude Stein's suggestion that Hemingway would return to Spain in July, this time with a heavily pregnant Hadley, to witness the annual running of bulls through the streets of Pamplona to celebrate the Fiesta of San Fermín. Both were instantly hooked on the event, loving the baroque religious processions, the endless parties and all-hours dancing of the traditional riau-riau.

Hadley readily concurred with Hemingway's decision to name their son – if the baby was a son – Nicanor Villalta Hemingway. In the event however, when their first-born finally arrived on October 10, they wisely

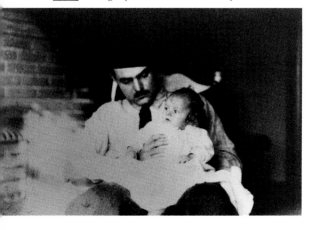

BELOW Hemingway with his son John (Bumby) in Paris, 1924

opted for the more prosaic John as his first name, adding only Villalta's forename to complete his birth certificate entry as "John Hadley Nicanor Hemingway." The sexually ambiguous "Hadley" was not only a tribute to his mother but also the alias Hemingway adopted for his journalistic moonlighting.

By this time the Hemingways were back in Toronto, called back to base by the new editor of The Toronto Star, Harry Hindmarsh. Hindmarsh did not like Hemingway, considering him too cocky and consequently assigned him to a series of mundane, insubstantial and inconsequential assignments in small provincial towns. Hemingway's response was to let loose a stream of four-letter epithets and to escape to Paris via regular correspondence with Gertrude Stein, Ezra Pound and Sylvia Beach, whom he helped by smuggling copies of James Joyce's *Ulysses* to American bookstores.

Intending to be present at his son's birth, Hemingway was enraged when he missed the event, being away in New York reporting on the arrival of Lloyd George. Back in Toronto he had a screaming row with Hindmarsh, telling him that "all work done by me from now on would be with the most utter contempt and hatred for him and all his bunch of masturbating mouthed associates."

From then, until he and Hadley cut loose from Toronto and returned to France on January 15, 1924, Hemingway's journalistic career would be spent back at the Star Weekly. Before that departure, however, Hemingway returned to Oak Park during the Christmas holidays. To his parents' disappointment, Hadley did not feel up to the trip, so they did not have the chance to meet their new grandson, now nicknamed "Bumby." Grace, however, was apparently mollified by the new-found maturity she believed fatherhood had bestowed on her wayward son. Among the gifts Hemingway took back to Toronto for Hadley was a package containing a little lace-trimmed frock for Bumby, a replica of the ones in which Grace used to dress his daddy.

Before leaving Oak Park, Hemingway slipped Marcelline (who had come from her new home in Detroit with her husband, Sterling Sanford) a copy of *Three Stories and Ten Poems*, making her promise not to let his parents see it. There is ample evidence that Marcelline, who expressed herself horrified by the "vulgar, sordid tale" he told in *Up In Michigan,* broke faith and passed it on to Ed and Grace who were, with some inevitability, similarly outraged.

With the financial safety net of employment with the Star whisked away from beneath him, Hemingway set sail from New York aboard the Cunard liner *Antonia* with nothing but a resolute determination to succeed as a creative writer. Whatever worries or doubts she may have harbored, Hadley was unflinchingly supportive. Both of them knew it was likely to be a long haul, but neither believed for a minute that the outcome would be anything but positive.

The publication of *Three Stories and Ten Poems* may not have set the literary world alight, but it represented the first flickers of a fame that Ernest Hemingway knew in his heart would come, and when it did come would be his by right.

ABOVE Hadley, Hemingway and Bumby, Austria 1926

fame, fortune

and tragedy

Scott Fitzgerald and Zelda

With a new apartment found at 113 rue Notre-Dame-des-Champs and Marie Rorbach, their former housekeeper, re-hired to give Hadley help with housework and looking after Bumby, Hemingway set about writing and searching for work.

Bumby was christened on March 16 at St. Luke's Episcopal Church. Chink Dorman-Smith, Gertrude Stein and Alice Toklas attended as godparents and the church choir included Giorgio, James Joyce's son. Bumby was dressed in the baptismal clothes worn by his father in 1899. Delighted godparents, Stein and Toklas would – a month later – buy Bumby a silver mug and rubber toys as christening presents, even taking their turn at wheeling him around the Luxembourg Gardens. Later, Bumby would describe them fondly as "the two giant women gargoyles" of his infancy, a description borne out by contemporary photographs.

The christening and ensuing party (with champagne and sugared almonds) was spoiled for Hemingway by the continued non-arrival of his copies of *In Our Time,* which was still being bound. That did not hamper the Transatlantic, which published a favorable review (by staff writer Marjorie Reid) in April, along with a brief paean of praise for *Three Stories and Ten Poems* by Kennon Jewett, another young staffer.

He would have to wait until October for the best, and most important, reviews of *Three Stories* and *In Our Time* to appear. These were the work of Edmund Wilson, and were published in The Dial only after Wilson badgered editor Alyse Gregory to use them, six months after they'd been submitted.

There was to be no sympathy in Oak Park when the five copies Ed and Grace Hemingway had ordered of *In Our Time* finally arrived from Bill Bird's office in Paris. Hemingway's parents were appalled by the subjects tackled, the tone of the writing and the liberal use of what they considered gross profanities. Doctor Ed was especially outraged by *A Very Short Story*, in which a soldier contracts gonorrhea from a salesgirl, and decided such filth had no place in his home. Despite Marcelline's warning that Ernest would be resentful if the copies were returned to Bird, all five were duly despatched.

Fast attaining the role of literary villain in Hemingway's life at Transatlantic Review was his boss, Ford Madox Ford. Far from following his stated aim of promoting the young and daring, Ford was now serializing *Some Do Not,* his own fictionalized war memoirs and, Hemingway was certain, writing pseudonomymous letters to the magazine extolling his own brilliance. Ford was hedging his bets, "running the whole damn thing as a compromise," Hemingway told Pound in a letter riddled with frustration.

That said, Ford had shown faith in Hemingway's work, publishing *Indian Camp* in the April 1924 issue and *The Doctor and The Doctor's Wife* and *Cross-Country Snow* at year-end, before Transatlantic finances ran out and Ford was forced to shut up shop. Hemingway had continued to push his favorites under Ford's nose with the result that the likes of

Ring Lardner, Donald Ogden Stewart, John Dos Passos and William
Carlos Williams featured in the magazine's pages during its brief year of
life. On June 4 Williams, a qualified and still-practising doctor, showed
his gratitude for the impending publication of his essay, *Voyage of the
Mayflower,* by circumcizing Bumby in the Hemingway's apartment,
forever after claiming that Ernest had almost passed out when he saw his
son's blood flowing.

Blood was definitely flowing by month end when Hemingway and
Hadley (no Bumby, who remained in Paris with Madame Rohrbach)
joined a merry bunch of friends in Pamplona. Taking up rooms in the
Hotel Perla, they included Bill and Sally Bird, Chink Dorman-Smith,
Donald Ogden Stewart, Robert McAlmon, George O'Neil, John Dos
Passos and his fiancée, Crystal Ross.

Besides the afternoon professional corridas, the menfolk (excepting
Dos Passos and Bill Bird, neither of whom shared Hemingway's passion
for the sport) regularly attended the amateur encounters held each
morning when aspiring Maeras and Villaltas could pit their passes and
wits against young bulls. Hemingway and Ogden Stewart both tried their
hand, Hemingway boasting five appearances in a letter to Pound, and
telling Edward O'Brien he'd been gored. He hadn't, of course, and the
one who had been hurt (suffering two fractured ribs and dented pride)
was Ogden Stewart, who headed back to Paris next day.

Hemingway's bravery in dashing in to aid Stewart was
rewarded by headlines in the Toronto Daily Star and the
Chicago Tribune. Of such things are legends made, and
Hemingway - happy to be a legend, if only for a day -
would not contact either to set the record straight.

At Bill Bird's suggestion the surviving members of the troupe moved
on to Burguete, a one-inn village set high in the Pyrenees, near the
Spanish-French border. An idyllic setting, it offered Hemingway a
myriad images for future reference, even if his mind was largely occupied
with work on *Big Two-Hearted River,* a story that he was determined
would bring a new collection to a fitting conclusion. Robert McAlmon
was staggered when a preoccupied Hemingway handed responsibility for
preserving Hemingway family fishing honors to Hadley, who dutifully
caught six in less than an hour.

Big Two-Hearted River was only one of 14 new stories Hemingway
would complete in 1924. Combined with the vignettes Bird had selected
for *In Our Time,* he saw them making "a good fat book" that he hoped a
U.S. publisher would take and promote properly. To that end he
recruited a number of friends and allies, including Donald Ogden
Stewart, Edmund Wilson, John Dos Passos, Sherwood Anderson and
Harold Loeb. None of them were able to interest either their own
publishers or any others in the collection.

It was an amended and abbreviated version of *Big Two-Hearted River*
which Horace Liveright – of the New York publishing partnership, Boni
and Liveright – read when Don Ogden Stewart gave him a typewritten

copy of *In Our Time*. Despite their refusal to publish it with the sexually explicit *Up In Michigan* included (so forcing Hemingway to hurriedly finish *The Battler*, a story about "a busted down pug and a coon"), and their offer of a relatively paltry advance of $200, Hemingway seized the chance with alacrity. He was, however, resolute that Liveright make no alterations to his texts without his approval, although he would bow to their greater knowledge of what was, and what was not, "acceptable" as far as any profanities and alleged obscenities were concerned.

Hemingway returned the signed Boni and Liveright contract and a copy of *The Battler* on March 31 confident that things were definitely on the up. Even if Liveright didn't do a great job promoting and selling *In Our Time*, he had proof that someone else wanted to publish him.

This had come in the form of an effusive letter from Maxwell Perkins, an editor at Charles Scribner's Sons, publishers of – among others – F Scott Fitzgerald.

This was, in fact, the second letter Perkins had written Hemingway, the first being misaddressed and so never reaching its intended destination. Given the correct address by John Peale Bishop, Perkins' second missive did arrive safely – but not before Hemingway had committed himself to the Liveright deal. Thinking on his feet, Hemingway made pointed reference in his reply to Perkins to the fact that Boni and Liveright had an option for his second and third books.

And so began one of the greatest writer–editor relationships of the modern world. Fifteen years older than Hemingway, Maxwell Evarts Perkins was a New York-born Harvard graduate (he studied economics) who had worked as a reporter on The New York Times for three years until 1910 when he joined Scribner's. Destined to become the company's vice-president and editor-in-chief, he worked tirelessly for and with his authors, among whom were Scott Fitzgerald and Thomas Wolfe, whose *Look Homeward, Angel* Perkins had converted from the confused unpublishable mess Wolfe had created into the masterpiece justly hailed as an American classic.

For now, Hemingway had every reason to feel content. *In Our Time* was going to be published in the U.S. by a major company. Another equally reputable publishing house was waiting in the wings. And he had been reunited with Bill Smith, the boyhood friend whose estrangement from Hemingway had been a severe blow.

Their reunion was as strange as any fiction. In April 1924 Hemingway had been in Arles when he chanced on a story in a Marseilles newspaper about a murder–suicide case back home in Chicago involving a former assistant district attorney, Wanda Stopa, who had tried to kill her lover, a publicist called Y.K. Smith, and his wife. It's impossible to say whether or not this coincidence was the prod Hemingway needed to start thinking about Bill and Katy Smith, but the following months were dedicated to putting many of those memories into words.

Biographer James Mellow is reasonably certain it "may have [also] prompted a steamy, incomplete Nick Adams story . . . never published during Hemingway's lifetime." It is not difficult to understand why. In the story in question, *Summer People*, Nick (nicknamed "Wemedge," one of Hemingway's youthful aliases) has anal intercourse with a girl Hemingway shamelessly named Kate. His description of their woodland coupling ("I love it. I love it. Oh, come, Wemedge. Please come . . . Please, please, Wemedge") was even more shocking than *Up In Michigan,* and shared its genesis with the same outpourings which produced two Bill Smith-related stories, *The End of Something* and *The Three-Day Blow.*

Hemingway, therefore, was thrilled when, sometime in November or early December, his mail included a letter from Bill, apologizing for the "savage, bitter" tone of the note he'd written to end their friendship and asking if they could, perhaps, "again capture some of what was once ours." The intervening years had not been kind to Smith who had suffered a nervous breakdown and manic-depressive episodes.

The two began corresponding at once, sending long, often bawdy and gossipy catch-up letters which did much to brighten Hemingway's mood. And when Bill Smith noted that Hemingway's mother was proud of him, Hemingway wryly explained that was only because "of the care with which I keep my printed works from the family fireside."

During a holiday in Schruns, Austria, Hemingway and Hadley hired a nurse to look after Bumby while they went skiing, camping out in a mountainside hut and escaping with nothing worse than a bad scare when high winds caused an avalanche which buried and killed four men. Back in the reality of a cold rainswept Paris, Hemingway pursued a friendship with Ethel Moorhead and Ernest Walsh – she a wealthy, middle-aged, severe-looking *pince-nez* wielding Scottish woman, he a gabby, young, thin lanky and tubercular American poet Hemingway had first met in 1922, at Ezra Pound's studio.

A genuine war hero who'd been badly injured in a plane crash, Walsh had been "adopted" by Ethel Moorhead who was now providing funds for a new magazine, This Quarter. The new title had already netted Hemingway 1,000 francs – then about $50 – for *Big Two-Hearted River,* which Walsh and Moorhead had accepted in January. Hemingway praised their policy of paying authors on acceptance and set about recruiting all the best writers he could, using Gertrude Stein as an unofficial, unpaid but very effective public relations officer.

After months of telling Bill Smith he should come to Paris, Hemingway had received word that his old buddy was planning to arrive in April. He suggested to Walsh that Bill take over his tasks, assuring Walsh that he could persuade Bill to do it for only $1,000 a month. Walsh's rejection of this plan included an implication that Hemingway was somehow trying to hit Moorhead for money. Surprisingly, Hemingway's friendship with Walsh survived this episode, although it didn't solve the immediate problem of what he and Hadley were going to do when Bill Smith arrived to find that there was no work for him.

Before that happened, however, there was the small matter of the first meeting of Ernest Hemingway and F. Scott Fitzgerald, two of the most distinctive voices in 20th Century literature, destined to become, and remain, the best of friends.

According to Hemingway in *A Moveable Feast,* their initial encounter took place at the Dingo bar some time in late April 1925. He was there

with, it's believed, socialite Lady Duff Twysden and her lover-cousin Pat Guthrie, while Fitzgerald was having a drink or six with Dunc Chaplin, a former Princeton University baseball star. Their conversation began well with Fitzgerald lavishing praise on Hemingway's work, but soured when he began asking impertinent personal questions about Hemingway and Hadley's sex life. Just as things were getting uncomfortably tense, Fitzgerald slumped, drunk and unconscious, to the floor. "That's the way it takes him," explained an unconcerned Dunc, helping Hemingway carry Fitzgerald to a taxi.

As fine and plausible as this tale is, Dunc Chaplin would deny being present at that meeting, pointing out that he did not visit Europe in 1925. During the next few months Hemingway and Fitzgerald would form a mutual admiration society based on a shared set of ideals concerning the direction of modern literature, discussing them in any bar or restaurant that happened to be handy.

Three years older than Hemingway, Francis Scott Key Fitzgerald hailed from St. Paul, Minnesota, the only son of an unsuccessful aristocratic father (through whom he was descended from and named for the composer of "The Star-Spangled Banner") and an energetic, although provincial mother. It was at Princeton that he first blossomed, becoming a leading light in the university's literary circle and The Triangle Club, a socially influential dramatic society, where he also formed what would be lifelong friendships with Edmund Wilson and John Peale Bishop, the poet-novelist he characterized as highbrow writer Tom D'Invilliers in *This Side of Paradise.*

Dropping out of Princeton after a failed love affair, Fitzgerald returned there briefly before joining the army in 1917. It was while based in Montgomery, Alabama, in 1918, that he fell in love with Zelda Sayre, daughter of a local Supreme Court judge. When the war ended, Fitzgerald had become a copywriter with a New York ad agency, been jilted by Zelda and retired home to St. Paul to rewrite a novel he'd begun in Princeton. Published by Charles Scribner's Sons in the spring of 1920, *This Side of Paradise* had been a huge hit. Its success and his newfound wealth soon persuaded Zelda to accept his renewed proposal of marriage.

In 1922 Fitzgerald matched the impact of his first novel with *The Beautiful and Damned,* the title perfectly describing him and his wife, both being hellbent on enjoying the fruits of his labors. These were – as he met Hemingway – about to blossom anew with the imminent publication of his most brilliant novel, *The Great Gatsby.*

If Hemingway and Fitzgerald hit it off from the start, Hemingway's first impressions of Zelda could not be described as good. Working with the advantage of 20/20 hindsight in *A Moveable Feast,* Hemingway claimed that he'd instantly diagnosed Zelda as clinically insane and, more dangerous perhaps, poisonously jealous of her husband's talent – the very thing which enabled her to enjoy the sybaritic lifestyle she so clearly enjoyed. For her part, Zelda was scornfully unimpressed by Hemingway's extravagant macho posturing ("Ernest, nobody is as male as all that"), a curt candor not guaranteed to warm him to her.

With the first edition of This Quarter (an issue dedicated by Walsh to the genius of Ezra Pound which included tributes from James Joyce and Hemingway, whose *Big Two-Hearted River* also appeared) finally ready to be printed, Hemingway was able to consider returning to Pamplona for the fiesta. Bill Smith, jobless, necessarily broke and a grateful house-guest in the Hemingways' apartment, was to be part of a much larger and more interesting crowd who would depart Paris for some fun, games and sexual intrigue under the Spanish sun. They were also, unwittingly, set to become the cast of Hemingway's first major novel, *The Sun Also Rises*.

Lady Duff Twysden (destined to be portrayed as Brett Ashley, arguably Hemingway's most potent fictional female and described as "A heavy drinker, promiscuous . . . [who] travels with an entourage of young homosexuals") would be there, inevitably accompanied by Pat Guthrie, an alcoholic bisexual who was to transmogrify into Mike Campbell, a gay beret-wearing drunk. Guthrie was nursing a grudge at Lady Duff's recent week-long liaison with American writer Harold Loeb.

During the Pamplona trip – which would become more fiasco than fiesta – Hemingway would come close to fisticuffs with Loeb, clearly jealous at his success with Lady Duff, a woman for whom he himself had developed a crush. Loeb, who'd be transparently characterized as the bald Robert Cohn, American writer and one-time Princeton boxing champion, all of which he was in real life, was not accompanied by Kitty Cannell, his mistress of the past three years and from whom he was trying to make a break. Not to be spared, she would appear, as Frances Clyne, in a section of the book set in Paris.

The Sun Also Rises

Don Ogden Stewart was in there too. Previously a committed homosexual (though the kind of "fairy" Hemingway, a vociferous homophobe, could presumably tolerate) he had recently embarked on his first heterosexual love affair with a Latin Quarter dancer known simply as Josephine. He and Bill Smith would be merged into the composite Bill Gorton for *The Sun Also Rises*.

All in all, sexual tensions were rife in Pamplona, not least because of the fascination Lady Duff had for the handsome young bullfighter, Cayetano Ordóñez (nicknamed Niño de la Palma) who had triumphed in a *mano a mano* encounter with the veteran Belmonte to become Hemingway's new hero and the matador character, Pedro Romero.

The narrator of *The Sun Also Rises* (entitled *Fiesta* in an early draft, the name it would be given when published in Britain) was Jake Barnes, a newspaper correspondent rendered impotent by severe war wounds.

Most of that first draft was written while he and Hadley travelled in Spain, visiting Madrid and Valencia among other locations, from where he wrote to various friends, including Bill Smith, to describe his progress with a book he was confident was going to "crack right through."

He was right, of course, but *The Sun Also Rises* was going to have to wait a while. At the end of that summer, and as the 1,335 copies of

LEFT A triumphant Pauline Pfeiffer

RIGHT Ed and Grace Hemingway with Ernest and Pauline in Key West, 1928

In Our Time were waiting to be released by Boni and Liveright with little promotion, Hemingway began to receive the first of many messages asking when they could expect delivery of the novel their contract demanded. Already unhappy with the company – they had corralled Sherwood Anderson, a recent arrival to their fold and enjoying great commercial success with his novel, *Dark Laughter*, into writing the jacket blurb which informed readers: "Mr. Hemingway is young, strong, full of laughter, and he can write" – he did not want to give them his work in progress.

Instead, while penning an insincere letter of thanks to Anderson for the blurb, Hemingway set about writing a novel which would not only savage a man he now believed had sold out but also stand no chance of being accepted by Boni and Liveright, whose hottest property Anderson had become. He would then be free to explore the possibility of a deal with Scribner's and others.

The result was *Torrents of Spring,* a book it took him only a week to write (from 23 to 30 November) and which Liveright, a month later, firmly rejected. Hemingway was free to start negotiations with Maxwell Perkins who, after prompting from Scott Fitzgerald and despite reservations among his colleagues at Scribner's, promptly accepted *Torrents of Spring* and set publication wheels in motion.

Its title, borrowed from a book by the Russian novelist Ivan Turgenev, *Torrents of Spring* was, in the words of critic and sometime Hemingway confidant Carlos Baker, "a satirical *jeu d'esprit* with a serious critical core and a mean streak down the middle." Set amid the smalltown provinciality of Petoskey, Michigan, and centred on the ramblings of a folksy character called Scripps O'Neil, that critical core would attack

Sherwood Anderson's *faux naiveté* and sentimentality, aim sideways digs at James Joyce's *Dubliners* and take hefty swipes at H.L. Mencken's habit of using "exotic" and always italicized foreign words and phrases to inject a touch of extra sophistication into the columns of The American Mercury. D.H. Lawrence was also satirized, while John Dos Passos' impressionistic style also popped up in humorous fashion, albeit more affectionately. But the most vicious aspects of the mean streak were reserved for Sherwood Anderson.

Just before Scribner's rush-released *Torrents of Spring* in May 1926, Hemingway wrote to Anderson explaining that, back in November, he'd been unable to resist an urge to give his former mentor a shove.

Reviews for *Torrents of Spring* were mixed but generally favorable. Allen Tate, who had loved *In Our Time,* considered the novella "a small masterpiece" which combined humor, ribaldry and satire in a way that made Hemingway "the best contemporary writer of 18th Century prose." For Ernest Boyd, another fan of *In Our Time,* Hemingway's future was now "immeasurably brighter," while the Chicago crowd – Anderson especially – were long overdue a good shaking. To Harry Hansen, however, Hemingway's strength lay in short stories and not in parody which was a gift of the gods he had not been granted.

The Second Marriage – Pauline

As if this wasn't exciting enough, Hemingway had another reason for feeling full of himself – he had, in April, begun a passionate affair with Pauline Pfeiffer, a Vogue fashion editor who'd wintered with the Hemingways at Schruns (Austria was still much cheaper than Switzerland). Hadley had learned of the affair from Pauline herself while they were sharing a trip along the course of the Loire and had, after the inevitable row with her husband, headed south with Bumby for the Cap d'Antibes estate of Gerald and Sara Murphy, a wealthy socialite couple who were now friends of Scott and Zelda Fitzgerald. Hemingway, for his part, headed for Madrid, early-season bullfights and writing – a trip which produced two important stories, *The Killers* and *Ten Indians.*

Hemingway had known Pauline and her sister Virginia ("Jinny") since he was introduced to them a year earlier by Harold Loeb's mistress, Kitty Cannell. Small and exotic in appearance, the sisters came from a very wealthy family. Their father had made his original fortune with a chain of drugstores in Missouri before buying 60,000 acres of farmland in north Arkansas and setting his tenants to delivering hugely profitable harvests of cotton, wheat and corn. Devoted Catholics, the Pfeiffers boasted a small chapel in their spacious farmhouse.

Pauline, who was the elder of the two vivacious sisters and four years older than Hemingway, had attended the Visitation Convent in St. Louis (where she'd been a contemporary and friend of Katy Smith – small world!) before majoring in journalism at the University of Missouri. She worked for a spell as a reporter on the Cleveland Star before becoming a fashion writer at the New York Daily Telegraph. Pressed

BELOW A scene from the 1957 film, *The Sun Also Rises* - starring Errol Flynn and Ava Gardner

ABOVE Errol Flynn runs through the Spanish streets during the bull-run sequence of *The Sun Also Rises*

by her family into an engagement to a lawyer cousin, Pauline had accept-ed her job as assistant to Mainbocher, Paris editor of Vogue, as an escape.

When they'd first met it had been Jinny who had caught Hemingway's eye, much to Pauline's relief. Her first impression was that he was a crude loafer. For his part, Hemingway was quick to realize that Jinny's sexual inclinations were exclusively sapphic and he would remain convinced that she had tried, on many occasions, to convert her sister to the arcane carnalities which so fascinated him.

Hemingway's affair with Pauline was no momentary lapse or whim, then, but a growing interest which became fascination. At last, inevitably, they found themselves in bed and in love. The depth of Hemingway's commitment towards Pauline can be gauged by the fact that he had openly begun to attend mass and told friends that he had, in fact, been a Catholic since a baptism ceremony held while he lay seriously injured in the Fornaci field hospital.

Arrant nonsense, of course. If he had been converted, Hemingway could never have married in a Methodist church and would have surely observed such Catholic customs as attending mass on Holy Days of Obligation. It's far more likely that he'd merely been given extreme unction by the priest who toured wards full of dead and dying men. Tellingly, Hemingway had made Jake Barnes a Catholic after initially giving that faith to Bill Gorton, so his growing attachment to Pauline had obviously begun to take hold in the summer of 1925.

Joining Hadley in Juan-les-Pins during June (the Fitzgeralds had given them permanent loan of a villa they'd rented but found uncomfortable), Hemingway asked for – but rejected – her suggestions regarding changes to *The Sun Also Rises*. Hemingway did, however, excise long biographical details about his principal characters which prefaced the novel and agreed

to various name changes which Maxwell Perkins suggested in a series of letters which passed between them.

Oddly, although it was terribly adult and sophisticated, Pauline Pfeiffer joined Hemingway, Hadley and Bumby at the villa, and travelled with them – along with the Fitzgeralds and Murphys – to Pamplona at month end. It was, of course, incredibly difficult for all concerned. By the end of that trip Pauline returned to Paris with the Murphys and the Hemingways announced their intention of separating. Sympathetic, Gerald Murphy gave Hemingway the keys to a studio flat he owned in Paris and deposited $400 in his bank account, ". . . [so] that when life gets bumpy . . . you are not hand-tied by the lack of a little money."

Murphy would receive a strange reward for his generosity. Many years later, when writing *A Moveable Feast,* Hemingway would (in a passage edited out of the published version) blame Gerald and Sara for his break-up with Hadley and eventual marriage to Pauline: ". . . I had hated these rich because they had backed me and encouraged me when I was doing wrong." Even at the end Ernest Hemingway was furiously re-writing his own history and desperately trying to pass the buck for his own considered actions.

As the October 22, 1925 release of *The Sun Also Rises* approached Hadley demanded, and got, an agreement that a three-month separation period should include lack of personal contact between Hemingway and Pauline. Reluctantly, Pauline agreed and headed back to Arkansas where she confided in her mother, Mary, whose first reaction was to ask how Hadley felt about things.

Hadley's divorce from Hemingway, on the grounds of his desertion, came through at the beginning of March 1927, by which time he had arranged with Maxwell Perkins that all book royalties from *The Sun Also Rises* were to be paid to her and Bumby in perpetuity. Finally admitting the true state of affairs to his parents after months of prevarication, he advised them that Hadley would be travelling in America with Bumby and wanted to visit Oak Park. The divorce was reasonably amicable, and not only for Bumby's sake, he stressed.

Hemingway and Pauline Pfeiffer were married on May 10, 1927, at L'Église de St-Honoré-d'Eylau, on Place Victor Hugo after he had returned from a trip to Italy with Guy Hickock (which Pauline wryly described as a "Italian tour for the promotion of masculine society") during which he was reunited with Ezra Pound and wrote an account of Mussolini's brave new state for The New Republic. He was not impressed, but enjoyed a vacation which took in Pisa, Florence, Forli, Bologna and Genoa and would also furnish him with material for a short story, *Che Ti Dice la Patria?* (What Does the Fatherland Say?).

During their honeymoon, which was spent in Grau-du-Roi, a village at the mouth of the River Rhône, Hemingway remained a dedicated notemaker, using it and Grau-du-Roi to supply the background for his uncompleted novel, *The Garden of Eden,* in which newlyweds David and Catherine Bourne skinnydip, eat great meals, make love luxuriously, both together and with an attractive young woman called Marita, to create a tangle of erotic experimentation and blurred gender roles.

All the while, Hemingway was finalizing the stories he and Maxwell Perkins had decided to include in a new collection planned for publication in October. A gathering of 14 stories – including the superb *In Another Country, Hills Like White Elephants* and *The Undefeated* (another masterful description of bullfighting) – *Men Without Women* also continued the Nick Adams/Hemingway saga with *Now I Lay Me*, in which Nick recalls the occasion when he helped his mother burn a pile of old junk they'd found in the basement. Had Ed's Indian trophies come back to haunt him?

Despite a lot of critical negativity for the collection Hemingway would be able to report to Scott Fitzgerald, in November, that *Men Without Women* had sold more than 7000 copies. By way of celebration he and Pauline (who was by now two months pregnant) planned a trip to Berlin, partly to view the annual six-day bicycle races and partly to visit his German publishers, Rowohlt.

On March 17 Hemingway had been able to advise Maxwell Perkins that he had been hard at work on a new novel, provisionally entitled *A New-Slain Knight* or, perhaps, *Jimmy Breen*. Variously described by Hemingway as a Tom Jones-style romp and his "Oak Park novel," he would abandon it after completing 22 chapters. As he readied himself to abandon Europe, Hemingway told Perkins that he was getting "a great kick out of the war and all the things and places and it has been going very well," probably the first reference he made to anyone else of the work that would result in *A Farewell to Arms.*

At the end of the month he and Pauline set sail for Cuba, on board the *RMS Orita,* leaving from the port of La Rochelle. From Havana they caught a smaller ship for Key West, then a busy fuel stop and harbor for Caribbean cruise ships, tramp steamers, car ferries plying between Florida and Cuba, and fishing boats, but a million miles away from the heaving tourist trap it is today. Biographer James R Mellow suspects that it may have been John Dos Passos who recommended the town to Hemingway, for he had visited it during a 1924 walking tour of Florida. Whoever it was, Hemingway was grateful – Key West was his kind of place.

Return to America – Key West

Renting an apartment on Simonton Street, Hemingway soon struck up acquaintance with people who would become life-long friends: Charles and Lorine Thompson, he a fisherman with whom Hemingway would enjoy many a sporting contest (and, strangely, never annoint with a nickname) whose family owned the local hardware store, ship's chandlery, tackle shop and a cigar box factory; and Eddie "Bra" Saunders, another fisherman and guide, whose boat Hemingway would rent when his first choice, the cabin cruiser *Anita* (owned by Josie Russell, the owner of Sloppy Joe's, the cave bar in which Hemingway would spend many happy hours) was employed in a contraband rum-run to Cuba.

As Pauline's pregnancy approached full term, she and Hemingway left Key West for Arkansas and the Pfeiffer homestead. It was from there, on

ABOVE Hemingway smiling and relaxed, at his favourite pastime – fishing in Key West, 1928

June 1, that Hemingway wrote to his father asking if he thought they should have the baby in Michigan. Ed advised against it, suggesting that they head for Oak Park Hospital where he would be happy to offer his services as obstetrician. Having received no reply, Ed wrote on June 18 urging Hemingway to respond "as we can make no plans to go to Windemere until I hear from you."

It was in the middle of a torrid heat wave, on June 27, that Pauline entered the Research Hospital in Kansas City to begin an 18-hour labor which ended with the Caesarean delivery of a nine-pound son she and her husband named Patrick. Her specialist warned them that Pauline should not consider having another baby for at least three years.

Before the move back to Key West took place, in late October Hemingway and Pauline (Patrick once more left in Piggott, Pauline obviously being neither a proponent or exponent of parent-child bonding) visited Oak Park where they found Ed Hemingway in even worse shape than before.

His Father's Suicide

Suspicious, tense and irritable, Ed had taken to locking his bureau drawers and become possessive of Leicester, even insisting that the 13-year old accompany him on his calls. Grace was frantic with worry and hurt by Ed's mistrust. It is possible, in hindsight, that he was trying to protect his wife from knowledge of the sorry state of his financial affairs.

Back in New York for a few days, Hemingway met up with Maxwell Perkins and spent time with Mike Strater and Waldo Peirce. Strater joined him and Pauline for a trip to Trenton, New Jersey, for the annual Princeton–Yale football game at Palmer Stadium and a long-overdue reunion with Scott and Zelda Fitzgerald.

After the game Scott Fitzgerald began drinking seriously, insulted a doctor on the train they all took to Philadelphia and grandly opened six bottles of Burgundy – intended solely for Hemingway – before dinner, a full evening dress affair. Drunk and increasingly obnoxious, Fitzgerald stunned everyone to embarrassed silence when he asked a young black maid: "Aren't you the best piece of tail I ever had? Tell Mr. Hemingway."

Settled into a white frame house Lorine Thompson had found for them on South Street, Hemingway, Pauline and Patrick were joined in Key West by Sunny. Unhappy as a dental nurse, Hemingway's sister had not needed too much persuading to become his typist, and Patrick's sometime nanny, as he began revising *A Farewell To Arms*.

Only two weeks after she arrived in Key West, Hemingway was off to New York to meet Bumby, who was coming from France to spend the Christmas–New Year holidays with his father.

After lunching with Maxwell Perkins on December 6, father and son were on board the train back to Florida when Hemingway received a telegram at the Trenton stop. It was from his sister Carol, telling him that Ed Hemingway was dead. Placing Bumby in the care of a Pullman porter and borrowing $100 from Scott Fitzgerald (he'd done his Christmas

shopping in New York and had only $40 cash on him), Hemingway caught the night train to Chicago.

Ed Hemingway had died from the shot he fired into his temple, using his father's old Smith and Wesson revolver to effect his departure from a world which he found increasingly unbearable. By all accounts he had awakened on the morning of December 6 with a severe pain in his foot – pain he would know, as a physician, could be due to arterial problems caused by his diabetes and could lead to gangrene and enforced amputation.

Although he had told Grace about the pain, he did not follow her advice to consult a colleague when he went to work at the hospital, as usual. Later, after lunch, he burned some personal papers in the basement before walking upstairs to the bedroom, closing the door quietly behind him.

It was Leicester, the son on whom he doted, who rushed in on hearing the shot and found his beloved father. Ed Hemingway was sprawled across the bed, blood oozing from the exit wound in his left ear. And it would be Leicester who Ernest, now most unwillingly the chief male of the family, sternly warned: "At the funeral, I want no crying. You understand, kid? There will be some others who will weep, and let them. But not in our family."

Leicester didn't. Neither did Hemingway, even if, as he told Maxwell Perkins in a letter written ten days later on Illinois Central Railroad stationery and postmarked Corinth, Mississippi: "What makes me feel the worst is my father is the one I cared about."

Ernest Hemingway was no longer a writer with wives and children to support. His mother, sisters and brother were also looking to him for help and sustenance as they struggled to make sense of Ed's suicide.

africa,

cuba, spain (1929-1938)

A Farewell to Arms

The publication of *A Farewell to Arms* on September 27, 1929 marked not only a milestone in modern American literature but also the arrival of a truly masterful author whose control of language, imagery and narrative was both exceptional and unique. It also marked the end of a year in which Ernest Hemingway had been forced to come to terms with his father's death and make a dutiful, if uneasy, peace with his mother.

This last was effected largely through financial support and never by reconciliation. After settling an unexpected tax bill of $578 that Grace had received, in February Hemingway promised to send her $100 a month for the next few years. Ed Hemingway had not, it transpired, left his wife a penniless pauper – his life insurance policy delivered $21,000, while there was a further $1,000 in various joint bank accounts. Invested by Grace this provided a further $100 a month income, the $200 total being ". . . all the difference between comfort and poverty" she wrote in a letter of thanks, which also stated her belief that, "Surely God will bless you when you have such a generous heart." The same letter promised that she would do her bit by taking in lodgers and resuming her career as a music teacher.

Handling the manner of Ed's death proved more difficult than paying tax bills and sending subsidies, however, and the subject would nag at Hemingway forever. Invariably painting his father as a coward both to friends and in his future writings, Hemingway nevertheless expressed some understanding of the emotional depths into which physical illness and financial problems had pushed him. There can be little doubt that he would have had his clearest understanding of Ed's last desperate act in the weeks before his own suicide.

Pursuing a strict work schedule on *A Farewell to Arms* (its title borrowed from a poem by the 16th Century English poet and dramatist George Peele), Hemingway nevertheless threw himself into his new-found passion for deep-sea fishing whenever possible, leaving Sunny and Pauline to type up the passages he'd revised in the mornings. In January, John Dos Passos stayed as house guest, and at month end Maxwell Perkins arrived, ready and willing to be introduced to the thrills of tarpon fishing and to take delivery of the manuscript.

On his way back to New York, on February 9, Perkins wrote a hurried note of thanks for his stay and described *A Farewell to Arms* as ". . . a most beautiful book" and the material as "immensely strong." Four days later he cabled Hemingway confirming Scribner's Sons offer of $16,000 for the serialization, advising him that some of the more uncompromising language ("fuck," "shit" and "cocksucker" included) would have to be replaced with blanks or abbreviations. Ever the pragmatist, Hemingway agreed, but only on condition that no changes or omissions be included without his approval.

In May, when Scribner's published the first instalment of *A Farewell to Arms,* Hemingway, Pauline, Bumby, Patrick and Sunny were en route for Paris. To his great dismay, Hemingway learned that Scott Fitzgerald

LEFT Gary Cooper and Helen Hayes in the 1932 film of *A Farewell to Arms*

PREVIOUS PAGE Hemingway and other war correspondents gather together in a trench, covering the Spanish Civil War

would also be there. Hemingway was reluctant to spend too much time with a man he knew could be very time-consuming and, worse, was apparently hellbent on destroying his art and what was left of his already fractured reputation.

Complete avoidance was impossible, of course, although Fitzgerald was apparently discomfited by the relative frostiness of Hemingway's greeting and hospitality when they were reunited.

Fractiousness between the two would climax during one of the afternoon boxing bouts Hemingway fought that summer in Paris with Morley Callaghan, a new Scribner's author.

On the day in question, Hemingway had lunched so well with Fitzgerald and John Peale Bishop it was decided the American Club gymnasium meeting would consist of one-minute rounds with two-minute breaks. Fitzgerald was to act as timekeeper.

In the first round, which seemed to Hemingway to go on forever, Callaghan caught him in the face with a couple of good shots. When Fitzgerald finally decided to called time, Hemingway was furious to learn that he'd let it go for almost four minutes. "If you want to see me getting the shit knocked out of me," he told an abashed Fitzgerald, "just say so. Only don't say you made a mistake."

Just before starting out on his annual tour of the Spanish bullfighting arenas, Hemingway heard that the second and third episodes of *A Farewell to Arms* had been banned in Boston, despite the abbreviation of swear-words and complete omission of sexually explicit passages. Writing to poet Archibald MacLeish from the home of Spanish painter Joan Miró in Montroig, Hemingway expressed fears that the controversy would encourage Scribner's to wield the blue pencil of censorship with even greater verve. He did not, apparently, consider the possibility that controversy can prove the most effective marketing and sales aid – which it most definitely did when *A Farewell to Arms* finally hit the bookstores of America.

The acclaim Hemingway received for *A Farewell to Arms* was everything he could have dreamed of, and more. This ranged from ". . . a moving and beautiful book" (from Percy Hutchinson in the New York Times Book Review) and ". . . the finest thing Hemingway has yet done" (Henry Hazlitt, New York Sun) to Malcolm Cowley's perceptive observation, in the New York Herald Tribune, that the title may be symbolic of ". . . Hemingway's farewell to a period, an attitude, and perhaps to a method also."

Also sobbing, with undisguised glee, were Scribner's Sons accountants. *A Farewell to Arms* sold its initial print run of 31,000 copies in a matter of weeks, with two reprints carried out in October and three more in November. Quick to cash in on its success, playwright Laurence Stallings acquired the stage rights (the resulting adaptation, starring Glenn Anders and Elissa Landi would run for only 24 nights when it opened on Broadway in 1930) while Paramount Pictures pitched in another $24,000 for the movie rights.

It would not be until 1932 that the first screen version of *A Farewell to Arms* was released, directed by Frank Borzage and starring Gary Cooper

BELOW A tragic war scene from *A Farewell to Arms*

and Helen Hayes. Cooper, with whom Hemingway would form a long and close friendship, was the author's first choice as leading man, but the cop-out happy ending Paramount executives inflicted on the story did not please him one bit.

Throughout his life, in fact, Hemingway remained supremely acidic about Hollywood's attempts to put his stories on the silver screen (although the money always came in handy), liking only the 1946 version of *The Killers* (starring Burt Lancaster, Ava Gardner and Edmund O'Brien) enough to keep a copy to watch at his home in Cuba.

Amid all the celebrations which filled that autumn came news that warranted the opening of another bottle of something special – in August John Dos Passos and Katy Smith had married, less than a year after their first meeting in Key West.

The Wall Street Crash of October 1929 emptied Paris of Americans for whom the main attraction had been the number of francs one could get for a dollar. The dollar, alas, was suddenly no longer almighty. The Hemingways were among those who headed home, this time with a French nursemaid, Henriette, accompanying Ernest, Pauline and Patrick on to *La Bourdonnais* when it sailed for New York on January 10, 1930. Allowing themselves a brief stay there, they sailed on to Havana before reaching Key West in early February, moving into a big house on Pearl Street. As before, Lorine Thompson had been their trusted home-hunter.

Hemingway did not publish much in 1930. It is known that he began work on a story, *The Sea Change,* which revealed Hemingway's continued fascination with female homosexuality. During the spring he also completed a wry and beautifully observed tale based on an encounter he and Bill Horne had had, with a couple of French roadside bootleggers during their 1928 hunting trip.

Wine of Wyoming would be published by Scribner's magazine that August and eventually take its place as part of the short-story collection *Winner Take Nothing*, as would *A Natural History of the Dead*, which recounted his first glimpse of wartime carnage in the gruesome aftermath of the explosion in the Milan munitions factory. Indeed, Hemingway would also use much of it – including the title – in his bullfighting epic, *Death in the Afternoon.*

Amending and rewriting *Death in the Afternoon,* he was also assiduously beginning to develop the new public image of himself, the artist as action hero, which was to become his trademark.

While his detractors would use this often vulgar persona to belittle Hemingway's literary achievements (apparently nobody with a beautiful soul could also have a hairy chest), it must be said that his own often crude references to homosexual writers and artists demeaned him every bit as much in the eyes of many. It was, in truth, the least attractive aspect of a man who could – and did – write the most beautiful, tender, evocative and sensitive stories.

This action-man myth-making received a kick-start in the spring of 1930 when Hemingway, Maxwell Perkins, John Herrmann (an old Paris acquaintance now living with his wife, Josephine Herbst, in Key West) and Mike Strater embarked on what was to be a four-day fishing and

ABOVE A page from a copy of *A Farewell to Arms* where Hemingway has filled in the blanks with his original words

Hemingway with his children, in Havana 1935

camping trip to Garden Key, one of the Dry Tortugas island group some 50 miles west, in the Gulf of Mexico. Trapped by a dramatic change in the weather they were forced to find shelter for two weeks in a tumbledown shed in an abandoned fort, eventually making their way back to a heroes' welcome.

Hemingway's plans to spend the summer in Spain were complicated by Pauline's announcement that she was pregnant once more. No matter, Ernest had to be in the heat and dust of the arena, and not merely to help him finish work he had on. He was as thrilled by bullfighting now as he had ever been, something he tried to explain to a puzzled Ezra Pound who chose to wrap it up with references to the ancient cult of Mithras. "I have never regarded bulls as anything but animals," he told him sternly. "I have never been a lover of animals. I have never heard of Mithra – lacking a classical education."

Hemingway left for Spain on May 2, travelling via Havana to Vigo on a ship filled with Spanish priests. Pauline was to follow with Patrick and the nanny a few weeks later, sailing from New York to Cherbourg and making her way to Hendaye Plage, south of Biarritz, for a brief holiday with her husband.

The Spain Hemingway rediscovered in the summer of 1931 was much changed from the country he had last seen two years earlier. Political unrest was fomenting following the departure into exile of King Alfonso in April, and the Second Republic now in place was proving a confusing mix of liberal ideals and conservative dogmatism which was being opposed, for hugely different reasons, by extremes as disparate as radical anarchists and the Catholic church. As rival factions fought their way

ABOVE Enjoying the sunshine and a drink on his terrace in Cuba

through elections for a new Cortes, Hemingway wrily advised Dos Passos in one of his letters home: "If worst comes to worst (sic) history of 1st Republic will repeat." Within five years his prediction would be proved remarkably accurate and Spain would be thrown into a bloody civil war.

For now, however, it was a time to immerse himself in the almost exclusively masculine society he so patently preferred to the more troublesome intricate one which included women. It has been observed many times that Hemingway's portrayals of men were invariably better observed, even more affectionate, than those of the women who appear in his stories. There may be something in Gore Vidal's contention that men like Hemingway (by no means unique in this respect) often attack those who are openly homosexual because they are aware of a similar inclination in themselves and are fearful of others seeing, or suspecting it.

Whatever the truth, the summer of 1931 saw Hemingway throw himself into the company of the bullfighting fraternity like never before. With Sidney Franklin at his side (the Brooklyn ace was recovering from a bad goring and had lots of time on his hands) he made a point of catching up with the new generation of fighters, and so was present in Madrid when Gitanillo de Triana – a young gypsy many believed capable of greatness – was gored in the spine. He died, agonisingly slowly, and some time later, of meningitis.

Prepared to lavish praise on bullfighters he considered masterful, graceful and brave, Hemingway was just as ready to condemn those who fell short of his enormously high expectations. Two men who came in for especial vilification in *Death in the Afternoon* were Cagancho (who had "not the courage of a louse") and Miguel Casielles ("a complete coward"). He had doubts, too, about Ignacio Sanchez Mejías's bravery, deciding that his posing and strutting was "as though he were constantly showing you the quantity of hair on his chest or the way in which he was built in his more private parts." Surprisingly, libel lawyers do not appear to have been employed in extracting retractions, apologies or hefty damages for these slurs.

On their way back to America on board the *Ile de France* in September, the Hemingways found themselves in the company of Donald Ogden Stewart and his wife, Beatrice, who, like Pauline, was pregnant. It was through the Stewarts that they were introduced to a young woman who was to play a decisive and destructive role in Hemingway's second marriage.

A strawberry blonde with startlingly blue eyes, Jane Mason was the 22-year-old wife of G. Grant Mason, head of Cuban operations for Pan American Airways and in every way Hemingway's ideal woman – beautiful, young and intelligent, she was not only a keen fan of deep-sea fishing and shooting but a talented amateur painter and sculptress.

By the end of the voyage Hemingway's interest in Jane had become fascination and if Pauline (who was no fool) failed to notice this, she can be forgiven for acceding to his suggestion that they invite the beautiful hoyden to Key West for a spot of fishing, rest and relaxation. It is more likely, however, that Pauline was perfectly aware of the *frisson* that had passed between Hemingway and Jane and decided that compliance was the best form of defence. If Jane was under her roof, she reasoned, Hemingway would surely not attempt a full-blown affair.

All these considerations were pushed aside in November when she and Hemingway headed for Kansas City for the birth of their new baby, duly baptized Gregory Hancock, after another long and painful labor which culminated in a Caesarean delivery. Gregory was, according to Hemingway in a letter he wrote soon after to Guy Hickock, a strapping nine-pounder with long arms and big feet. "Hope the bastard has a talent for business," he added.

Revisions to *Death in the Afternoon* were Hemingway's main preoccupation over the next six months, however, including taking John Dos Passos's advice to make substantial cuts to his original text.

While he praised much of the book as "a knockout" and "an absolute model for how that sort of thing ought to be done," Dos Passos had serious reservations about long passages discussing literary life, the creative writing process and Hemingway's paeans of praise for Key West – all of which he described candidly as "unnecessary tripe." In his reply, Hemingway admitted that he had, after going over the book numerous times, "cut 4 1/2 galleys of philosophy and telling the boys" and reduced Chapter 20 to the section paying homage to Spain and its people.

Published on September 23, 1932, *Death in the Afternoon* was a far greater critical success than might have been expected for a book that dealt mostly with a sport which a fair number of Americans considered barbaric. Many, inevitably, elected to concentrate on the ways in which it reflected what they knew (or had been told) of its author's personality – or his carefully cultivated image.

Granville Hicks (of The Nation) was convinced, for example, that the book was likely to sell on the strength of that image rather than any real interest in or sympathy with its subject. Lincoln Kirstein (in Hound & Horn) wrote that it stood "head and shoulders above his worst self; it is his best self . . ." And Hershel Brickell (writing in the New York Herald Tribune) found it "excellent reading, full of the vigor and forthrightness of the author's personality, his humor, his strong opinions – and language." In short, he concluded, *Death in the Afternoon* "is the essence of Hemingway."

It would be a full ten months (in the June 7, 1933 edition of The New Republic) before a truly negative review appeared, and one which Hemingway perceived as an attack on his masculinity and sexuality. Written by Max Eastman, who had obviously bought into the canard being spread by Robert McAlmon – that Hemingway was a closet gay and wife-beater – it declaimed the "unconscionable quantity of bull" written into the bullfighting sequences before suggesting that it was "a commonplace that Hemingway lacks the serene confidence that he is a full-sized man. . . . Some circumstance seems to have laid upon Hemingway a continual sense of obligation to put forth evidences of red-blooded masculinity."

Worse, even if it was very clever, Eastman picked up on the dismissal of Ignacio Sanchez Mejías's posturing to describe Hemingway's school of "new" fiction writing as "a literary style, you might say, of wearing false

BELOW Jane Mason with her husband and two sons in Havana

hair on the chest." The repercussions would resound for some time and even though The New Republic refused to publish furious ripostes from Hemingway and Archibald MacLeish, it did print a denial of innuendoes by Eastman who also wrote pacifying letters to both men. Unimpressed, Hemingway described Eastman as "a slimy lying shit" and vowed to deliver the most basic type of revenge if their paths crossed.

Despite Leicester Hemingway's memories of the spring of 1933 (which, as anyone who has read his *My Brother, Ernest Hemingway* can attest, were blessed with 20/20 hindsight vision through rose-tinted spectacles), there is no doubt that Jane Mason and Ernest Hemingway enjoyed an affair which hurt Pauline dreadfully.

Taking off for Cuba with increasing regularity (Josie Russell's cruiser, *Anita,* boasted a log entry "Ernest loves Jane") ostensibly for fishing expeditions, he forced an abject letter from Pauline at one stage which included news that she had been trying out new hairstyles and "Am having large nose, imperfect lips, protruding ears and warts and moles all taken off before coming to Cuba." Pushing her point home with a further attempt at humor, she added: "Thought I better, Mrs. Mason and those Cuban women are so lovely."

Jane Mason ensured that Pauline could relax a little when, in late May, she first crashed her car (in which Bumby, Patrick and her adopted son, Antony, were passengers) on her way to the Mason estate at Jaimanitas. Although all escaped unscathed, Jane went into a depression and a few days later fell (or jumped) from an upper-floor balcony and broke her back. Shipped back to New York for treatment she would spend five months in hospital and a full year in a back brace.

His principal diversion out of the way and yearning for new thrills, Hemingway set his sights on visiting the biggest game-park he could imagine – Africa. Uncle Gus Pfeiffer shared his dream to the extent that he committed himself to underwriting a safari to the tune of $25,000, some of which Hemingway dedicated to commissioning a custom-made Springfield rifle with telescopic sight.

Charles Thompson, Archie MacLeish and Mike Strater had been his initial choices as companions for this new great adventure, but MacLeish and Strater – both of whom had experienced his ferocious competitiveness on fishing trips – regretfully declined, offering prior commitments as their excuse.

Charles, however, was up for it and fell in with what soon became quite complicated plans. Hemingway, Pauline, her sister Jinny, Bumby (who was staying with them while Hadley remarried in London) and Patrick would leave for Spain early in August, leaving Gregory with his nursemaid, Ada. While Hemingway followed the bullfight "caravan," the others would go on to Paris. It was there, in October, that Charles would join them and from there that he, Hemingway and Pauline would set off for Africa.

Hemingway's summer in Spain proved to be a distressing experience for a man who depended on a *status quo* to freeze his memories in aspic. Nothing was as he last saw it, it seemed to him. The political situation was, if possible, worse than before with government graft and greed endemic. There were too many fingers in the pie, he told Mary Pfeiffer, his mother-in-law, in a letter. And when the plums ran out there would be a revolution.

Hemingway's despondency may be attributed to the fact that reviews for the newly-published short-story collection, *Winner Take Nothing,* had only been so-so. He was also perturbed by what he perceived as Scribner's lack of follow-up advertising support for the collection and the publishers' apparent dropping of *Death in the Afternoon* after what had seemed a promising start.

Paris, to his dismay, was not much better than Madrid had been. A number of friends were dead, he learned, while old haunts had either been taken over by middle-class Parisians or were now filled with Germans escaping the ascendant Nazi regime.

The return was not all unremitting gloom, however. Sylvia Beach still reigned supreme at Shakespeare and Company, her welcome genuine and fulsome. Janet Flanner, Paris correspondent of The New Yorker, was similarly glad to see him, while Solita Solano, her partner, readily offered to type up the (long) short story Hemingway had begun writing in Spain. Set in Cuba, *One Trip Across* introduced the rum-running adventurer Harry Morgan and would form the framework on which he would build the novel *To Have and Have Not.* Forwarded to Cosmopolitan magazine in New York, *One Trip Across* would be published in April 1934 and reap him $5,500 – a formidable amount, which equates to about $47,000 in today's terms.

The Great White Hunter

On their last night in Paris, Hemingway and Pauline gave a dinner for James and Nora Joyce, at which Nora jokingly suggested that her husband would benefit from "a bit of that lion hunting." Joyce (whose spectacle lenses were as thick as a submarine's portholes) pointed out that he'd be unable to see the quarry, let alone aim an accurate shot at it. Hemingway promised Joyce he would return with a live specimen. "Fortunately," Joyce recalled wryly, "we escaped that."

The trip began promisingly well. After reaching Kenya and the hill farm of Philip Percival near Machakos, south of Nairobi, they'd spent a few weeks shooting gazelles, impala and guinea fowl on the nearby Kapiti Plains. Hemingway liked his white hunter guide at once. A British military intelligence veteran who reminded him of Chink Dorman-Smith, Percival had hunted with Teddy Roosevelt when young, was a crack shot and – most importantly – fully understood animal psychology and behavior patterns.

With two equipment trucks, a white mechanic and local Kikuyu tribesmen as beaters, gun-bearers and caterers, the party moved 200 miles south into Tanganyika (now Tanzania). They established camp at Arusha on the edge of the vast Serengeti Plain, in time to spend Christmas Day camping in a beautiful wilderness filled with millions of migrating wildebeest and attendant predators – hyenas, vultures and

lions, the trophy that Hemingway coveted the most. To his chagrin, the first lion he killed was credited by the bearers to Pauline, who had clearly missed with her shot.

When Hemingway was incapacitated by amoebic dysentery he was forced to suffer two days of agony before a light two-seater plane, the *Puss Moth,* arrived to take him back to Nairobi for treatment.

Laid up in Nairobi's New Stanley Hotel, Hemingway made a number of fascinating new acquaintances, among them Bror Blixen, the celebrated white hunter and ex-husband of Karen Blixen whose writings (under the *nom de plume* Isak Dinesen) would be the inspiration for the 1985 Robert Redford-Meryl Streep movie *Out of Africa.* Blixen's current socialite client was Alfred Vanderbilt, one of Jane Mason's friends. The world was still shrinking.

Back at a new base camp, on the edge of the vast Ngorongoro Crater, Hemingway's luck did not improve. Now hunting rhino and kudu, a horned antelope, he found himself consistently out-gunned by Charles Thompson whose haul of rhino and kudu horns always managed to be longer, bigger and thicker. It had been a memorable safari, though not always for the right reasons, and Hemingway vowed to return one day.

It was a promise he would repeat to the journalists who pressed around him in New York when he and Pauline returned from France on the liner *Paris* at the end of March. Of equal interest to New York's press pack was another passenger with whom Hemingway had formed an instant friendship destined to last many years – actress Marlene Dietrich, a woman he affectionately nicknamed "the Kraut."

While he told reporters that his priority was to return to Key West and knuckle down to writing, which would pay for his next safari, his mind was really fixed on finalizing the purchase of a 38-foot cabin cruiser from a Brooklyn boatyard. The $3,300 deposit for the $7,500 craft came from Arnold Gringrich of Esquire magazine, as an advance against future articles. When the boat was delivered to Key West a month later, it bore the name *Pilar,* partly in homage to the shrine of Nuestra Señora del Pilar in Zaragoza, but also in honor of the alias Pauline had used in the cables she'd sent during his separation from Hadley.

There was an unhappy reunion with Scott Fitzgerald in New York, at which Fitzgerald was too drunk to be coherent. Writing to Maxwell Perkins a few weeks later, Hemingway criticized Fitzgerald for drawing too much on Gerald and Sara Murphy as models for his central characters, transforming them into himself and Zelda, but had not made them act in ways in which a couple like that would have behaved.

Wisely keeping such hurtful personal observations to himself when he finally replied to Fitzgerald's request for a no-punches-pulled critique of *Tender Is the Night,* Hemingway nevertheless told his friend that he had ". . . cheated too damned much on this one. And you don't need to." Ramming his point home, Hemingway added: "You can write twice as well now as you ever could. All you need is to write truly and not care what the fate of it is."

Time heals, they say, and distance lends insight. A year later, Hemingway informed Perkins that, with rereading, *Tender Is the Night*

BELOW Hunting in Tanganyika – 1934

ABOVE A poster for the 1952 film *The Snows of Kilimanjaro*, starring Gregory Peck and Ava Gardner

"gets better and better. I wish you would tell him I said so." Perkins did and Fitzgerald, touched and gratified, pasted the note in his scrapbook.

Much of 1934 was spent working on the manuscript of what would emerge, in 1935, as *The Green Hills of Africa*. Like *Death in the Afternoon*, this hymn to southern Africa, its scenery, wildlife and the thrill of hunting would be weighted down with Hemingway's thoughts on literature, the art of writing and some of its leading practitioners. He ought, perhaps, to have remembered Dos Passos's counsel regarding similar passages in the Spanish book, excised or reduced them and stuck to what made parts of *The Green Hills of Africa* memorable – the lavish descriptions of the countryside and its wild inhabitants.

He didn't, so the reviews which greeted its publication were lukewarm at best and harshly critical on a number of occasions. Worst, to Hemingway's mind, was Edmund Wilson's long essay in the December 1935 issue of New Republic which said, *inter alia*, that it was the only book he'd seen which made Africa and its animals seem dull, that Hemingway's adoption of first-person narrative seemed to coincide with a loss of self-criticism. Wilson did not doubt Hemingway's ability, but he wished he would return to fiction, the thing he did best.

Towards the end of 1934 Hemingway had, in fact, begun to do just that. His affair with Jane Mason was briefly resumed but abandoned when she took up with sportsman and elephant hunter Richard Cooper. He made a start on a new story, *The Short Happy Life of Francis Macomber*, and is thought to have made preliminary notes for *The Snows of Kilimanjaro*. Mason, by the way, would go on to have an affair with Esquire editor Arnold Gringrich, news of which threw Hemingway into a furious rage, not with Mason but with Gringrich.

The Short Happy Life of Francis Macomber was an account of a wealthy sportsman's cowardice when confronted by a lion and the revenge his disgusted wife takes by sleeping with their hired game hunter. Later, when Macomber is charged by a rhino, and given the chance to redeem himself, it is an errant shot from his wife's rifle that kills him.

Good as *Macomber* was, *The Snows of Kilimanjaro* explored similar territory in much greater depth and to far greater effect. The story of a writer, Harry Walden, who is dying from a gangrene infection in the foothills of Africa's tallest mountain, it recalls details of Walden's often stormy marriage told in flashback as his wife, Helen, keeps watch for the plane which is to carry him to hospital. Never collapsing into pathos or melodrama, *Kilimanjaro* was a wonderfully incisive portrayal of the cuts and scars people can inflict on each other when a marriage turns sour.

To Walden/Hemingway (there is too much of the author in Walden to be divisible from him), his wife's wealth had made him loose, sloppy and indolent. Their safari was his bid to regain some of the powers he'd had as a young man in Paris before marriage, comfort and luxury had dulled his creative edge. In his dying moments he calls Helen a "rich bitch." Given the autobiographical source of much detail, *The Snows of Kilimanjaro* was a pretty hefty can of worms for Hemingway to open, but all the more powerful for that. To jumble and mangle metaphors, Hemingway really was washing his and Pauline's dirty linen in public.

The winter of 1935–36 was a grim one for Hemingway. Gloom at poor sales for *The Green Hills of Africa,* the onset of a mild case of writer's block, his unhappiness with the way his marriage was drifting, and his concern for Scott Fitzgerald's increasing decline into alcoholism and despair, all combined to drag him into what he told Dos Passos was ". . . that gigantic bloody emptiness and nothingness, like I couldn't ever fuck, fight, write and was all for death."

Death of a different kind was the fascination which pulled him out of his blues. Since he'd discovered the joys of fishing for tuna in the waters off Bimini, the tiny island complex some 50 miles east of Miami, Hemingway had also become fixated with the sharks which made that sport so spectacular. Katy Dos Passos was present when, after a long battle to reel in a giant tuna, Hemingway had been forced to watch helplessly as sharks moved in to steal it.

That battle, which Hemingway claimed was the norm for fishermen in shark-infested waters, had an echo in a story he was told about this time by Carlos Gutierrez, the 53-year-old Cuban he'd hired to skipper the *Pilar.* According to Carlos, an old man fishing alone in the Gulf Stream had hooked a huge marlin which pulled his skiff out to sea for two days and nights. Eventually he had managed to haul it in and lash it to his boat, only for sharks to home in. Exhausted by his attempts to fight them off, the old man was finally rescued by fellow fishermen. Half his catch had been devoured, but that half still weighed 800 lbs. It was a magnificent and thrilling story – and one that Hemingway filed away for future reference.

A key element of *The Snows of Kilimanjaro* was the character Harry Walden's memories of Paris and the many ways in which some of his contemporaries had been sucked in by the siren voices of the rich, their early promise betrayed by success and indulgence. Amazingly, Hemingway elected to use his friend Scott Fitzgerald as an example of that process.

As brutal as it was condescending, that judgement was bound to offend Scott Fitzgerald when Esquire published it in August 1936. His protest letter, mailed from North Carolina where Zelda was undergoing another course of treatment, was surprisingly mild given the severity of the slight, and in it he requested that Hemingway cut out his name if and when the story was incorporated in a book. "Riches have never fascinated me," he added in a postscript, "unless combined with the greatest charm or distinction."

Perhaps, given the undercurrents present in "Macomber" and "Kilimanjaro," his row with Fitzgerald and his own recent depression, Hemingway was ready to move on, as far as personal relationships were concerned, by the end of 1936. If so, Martha Gellhorn happened along at precisely the right time. Twenty-eight years old, tall, blonde and attractive, she was a published author whose narrative skills had been favorably compared to Hemingway's and had extensive first-hand knowledge of Europe, especially France, Germany and Spain.

Martha Gellhorn was born and raised in St. Louis where her father was an eminent gynaecologist and her mother an active suffragist and social worker. Martha had been educated at Bryn Mawr before having work published by The New Republic, the St. Louis Post-Dispatch and the French edition of Vogue. Her first novel, entitled *What Mad Pursuit*, had featured the epigraph, "Nothing ever happens to the brave," which was in actual fact a line of Hemingway's.

They met one afternoon late in December when Martha, who was vacationing in Key West with her mother and brother, Alfred, dropped in to Sloppy Joe's for a drink. She and Hemingway struck up a conversation which went on long into the evening and ruined a dinner party Pauline was giving that night.

Staying on in Key West after her mother and brother's holiday came to an end, Martha became something of a permanent fixture in the Hemingway residence on Whitehead Street. She managed to form a reasonably amiable relationship with Pauline, although the latter was understandably wary. Martha was later given Hemingway's unconditional seal of approval by being asked to read and comment on the draft of his new work-in-progress – the Harry Morgan novel *To Have and Have Not*.

BELOW Humphrey Bogart and Lauren Bacall in a famous scene from *To Have and Have Not*

The Spanish Civil War

Their mutual affection for Spain played a part in cementing their initial relationship and undoubtedly filled many of their early conversations. Since July, when the Governor of the Canary Islands, General Francisco Franco, had led a military revolt which culminated in his proclamation as *generalissimo* of "Nationalist" Spain in October and the recognition of Adolf Hitler and Benito Mussolini, Spain had been immersed in the civil war Hemingway had long predicted as inevitable.

With Madrid under siege by Franco's forces, Martha (who had pretty soon been nicknamed "Marty") had already been asked to cover the conflict for NANA, the North American Newspaper Alliance. The day she left Key West for St. Louis, Hemingway suddenly announced that he had to go to New York the next day. He met up with Martha in Miami and travelled with her as far as Jacksonville, where their routes diverged. In New York Hemingway contacted NANA and volunteered his services as a correspondent in Spain. Since Hemingway's bona fides as a newspaper writer and an expert on Spanish affairs were unrivalled and his by-line a coup any editor would die for, NANA chief John Wheeler accepted his proposal with alacrity.

He then returned to Key West and, finishing work on his new novel, informed Pauline of his plans, persuading her that accompanying him was impossible. On February 27, 1937 he and Sidney Franklin, the bullfighter he had recruited as a helpmate, embarked for France. Martha Gellhorn was in New York, still trying to arrange fake credentials to travel in Spain as a supposed correspondent for Collier's magazine.

Hemingway's credentials were in order and he was able to file his first story – an account of a fierce battle in and around the town of Brihuega in which Loyalist Republican troops had defeated an Italian force – on March 22. Although the Loyalists were, and would remain, a poorly trained, ill-equipped and politically divided raggle-taggle band compared to the German- and Italian-backed rebel Nationalists of General Franco, all of Hemingway's natural inclinations made him a consistent propagandist for their cause. In this he was as one with all the liberally inclined correspondents in whose company he found himself. These included the photographer Robert Capa, New York Times correspondent Herbert Matthews and Joe North, editor of New Masses.

NANA duties apart, Hemingway was also involved in the making of *Spanish Earth*, a pro-Loyalist documentary he co-produced with John Dos Passos, Lillian Hellman and Archibald MacLeish, for which he wrote and recorded the sparse but telling narration.

Completing revision work on *To Have and Have Not,* Hemingway returned to Madrid and Martha, with whom he was now openly having an affair. With the capital much quieter as the war raged unabated elsewhere, Hemingway found time to capture the time, place – and Martha – in his first and only play, *The Fifth Column.* The woman correspondent in the play, Dorothy Bridges, is obviously Martha

ABOVE Hemingway contemplating the dead soldiers in Madrid

LEFT A puff of smoke mushrooms into the sky after an air raid by General Franco's bombers

Gellhorn just as Philip Rawlings, big, brave, boozy and working undercover as a spy, is a typical Hemingway wish-projection of himself.

The publication, in October 1937, of *To Have and Have Not* was not an excuse for celebration and flags, though sales were reasonable. Where the Harry Morgan short stories had been tight, punchy and well-constructed pieces, *To Have and Have Not* wandered off, again, into Hemingway's old habit of settling scores with friends and rivals.

As the tide began to turn inexorably against the Loyalists in 1938, Hemingway joined with John Whitaker of the New York Herald Tribune and Edgar Mowrer of the Chicago News to advise Claude Bowers, the U.S. Ambassador, that he should make contingency plans to evacuate American patients and medical staff from Spanish hospitals.

During his final visit to Spain during the civil war, Hemingway was witness to the horrendous Battle of the Ebro, during which an estimated 70,000 Loyalists were killed on that river's banks. On November 15, in Barcelona, the volunteers of the International Brigade were given a farewell parade and told by the Communist firebrand Dolores Ibarruri – "La Pasionara" – "You can go proudly. You are history. You are legend." The war was all but over and Franco had emerged victorious.

In February 1939, Hemingway's bitterness at Franco's victory became public in an issue of New Masses. Paying homage to those who had fallen in battle, and continued to do so as remnants of the Republican Army retreated, he wrote: "The dead sleep cold in Spain tonight and they will sleep cold all this winter as the earth sleeps with them. The dead do not need to rise. They are part of the earth now and the earth can never be conquered . . . It will outlive all systems of tyranny."

for whom

the bell tolls (1939-1945)

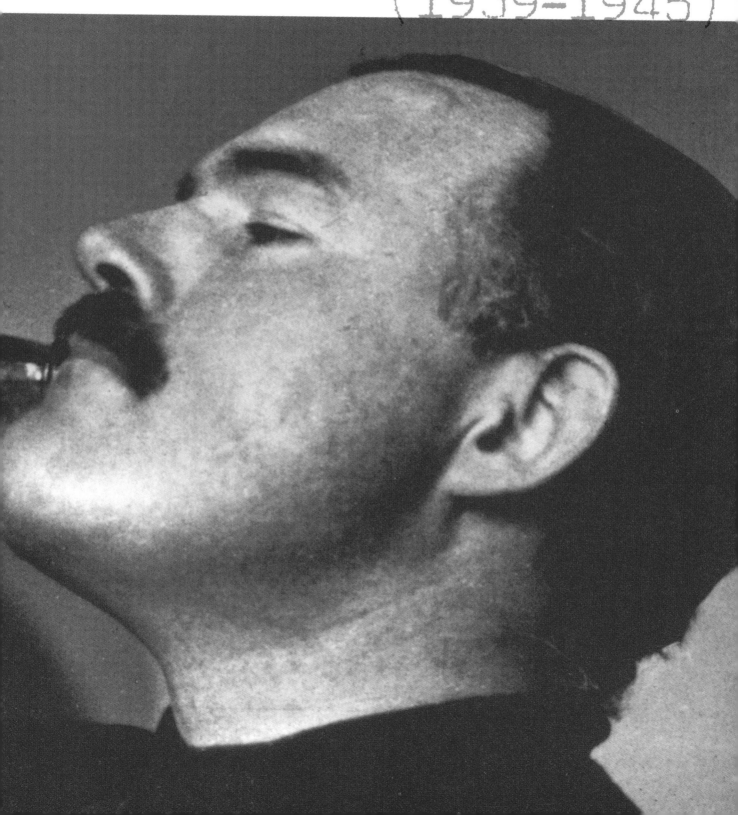

Marriage to Martha

In July 1939 Hemingway wrote a long letter to Hadley in Paris, partly to confirm that he planned to spend part of the summer with Bumby, Patrick and Gregory in Wyoming, and partly to tell her he had "never worked harder nor steadier" than during the past six months. So far he had 58,000 words written on 340 manuscript pages, but he wanted to finish it before Adolf Hitler's remorseless bellicosity precipitated a war in Europe. The book was, of course, *For Whom the Bell Tolls* and its importance to Hemingway cannot be underestimated. As he told another old friend, the socialite sportsman Tommy Shevlin: "It is the most important thing I've ever done and it is the place in my career . . . I have to write a real one."

That he had been able to achieve so much is testament to Hemingway's ability to compartmentalize his life so thoroughly, to cut off from reality, for the recent past had been filled with enough diversions to stop one of Hitler's Panzer divisions in its tracks, let alone a man embarked on a task which ought ideally to be conducted with as few outside interruptions as possible.

Plagued by nightmares of the Loyalist retreat from the Elbo in the weeks following his return to Key West, he had briefly put the novel aside to work on some short stories but soon steeled himself to tackle a book in which he would attempt to "write understandingly about . . . deserters and heroes, cowards and brave men, traitors and men who are not capable of being traitors." This was the ambition that he outlined to Ivan Kashkin, Russian translator of his New Masses article, in March when the nightmares had finally begun to fade and his pen began scurrying anew.

Shuttling between Key West and the refuge of his room at Havana's Hotel Ambos Mundos, Hemingway maintained his strict work-play schedule which consisted of mornings at his desk and afternoons on the *Pilar,* chasing whatever game there was to chase. His relationship with Pauline had become increasingly tense – another reason to flee Key West – while Martha had set herself up in Havana where she was working on short stories and *The Stricken Field,* a novel inspired by her relationship with Hemingway. In this she was war correspondent Mary Douglas and he was known simply as John.

Dissatisfied with arrangements at the hotel, Martha found Finca Vigía, a run-down farmhouse with 15 acres of land in the village of San Francisco de Paula, not far from the capital. Boasting a watchtower and swimming pool, its $100 a month rent seemed steep to Hemingway, whose notorious parsimony remained intact. Martha took it on anyway, paying for renovations herself. When these were finished Hemingway moved into Finca Vigía, keeping the hotel as his mailing address in order to maintain a semblance of propriety even though a growing number of intimate friends knew precisely what the deal really was. He was aided greatly in this pretence when Pauline decided to spend that summer in Europe with friends.

Although he and Pauline would try to keep the protracted negotiations of their inevitable divorce as reasonable as possible, if only for Patrick and Gregory's sakes, Gregory would have clear memories of shouting matches, crying fits and door-slamming departures during the months in which the couple eventually settled on a divorce suit on the grounds of Hemingway's desertion. No mention of adultery, which would have been scandalous, and Pauline was to have custody of the boys. However, Hemingway would enjoy full uncomplicated access to his sons and continue his practice of taking them on extended summer trips.

All this dragged on while work proceeded on *For Whom the Bell Tolls,* a task made lighter by Maxwell Perkins's undisguised enthusiasm for the project early in 1940 when Hemingway forwarded him typewritten drafts of the first few chapters from Havana. "It is truly wonderful," Perkins confirmed. "The first chapter, or the first eight pages, had the old magic . . . Well, of course I am mighty impatient to see more."

A few months later, when Hemingway had delivered more than 500 pages to Scribner's, Perkins could tell him: "I think this book has greater power, and larger dimensions, greater emotional force, than anything you have done . . . It is an astonishing achievement . . ." It was the sort of praise any author craves and enough to keep Hemingway hard at work.

The great workload, combined with long hard fishing trips and heavy drinking, would hit Hemingway hard in April, however. Writing to give Perkins a progress report, he admitted that he had been laid up for five days: "My heart was only hitting 52 [beats a minute] at noon and Dr said I was shot with over-work and should lay off for two months or so. Stayed in bed 2 days. Loafed three and went back to work last Wednesday."

LEFT Hemingway and his son relaxing in the Idaho sunshine

BELOW The 1943 film, *For Whom The Bell Tolls,* starring Ingrid Bergman and Gary Cooper

ABOVE Hunting in Sun Valley, Idaho, 1940

As publication day loomed Perkins could confirm that the Book of the Month Club were to make *For Whom the Bell Tolls* their main selection (which meant a club edition of 135,000 copies), while Scribner's intended to go with a first edition print run of 160,000. By April 1941 U.S. sales totalled 491,000 copies – by any standards a bestseller. Even better, in financial terms at least, Paramount would come up with a very acceptable offer of $136,000 for the film rights – just over $1 million today. Even better than that, director Sam Wood readily agreed to cast Hemingway's preferred actor, Gary Cooper, in the lead role of Robert Jordan, a former professor of Spanish at the University of Montana who is the dynamite expert for an International Brigade group of guerrillas. Hemingway had delivered "the real one."

According to reviewers and the book-buying public of America and Britain (where his publishers, Cape, had a huge success despite production problems caused by wartime paper rationing), *For Whom the Bell Tolls* was a phenomenal book in every respect. While he was doubtless pleased by the praise lavished by such publications as The New Yorker ("I do not much care whether or not this is a 'great' book. I feel that it is what Hemingway wanted it to be: a true book" – Clifton Fadiman) and the New York Times (". . . the best book Hemingway has written . . . It will, I think, be one of the major novels in American literature" – J Donald Adams), Hemingway must have been on tenterhooks until word came from the Olympian Heights of The New Republic and the wisdom of Edmund Wilson, whose stern judgements had pricked many a previous celebration party balloon, was delivered.

Wilson's considered view was that "Hemingway the artist is with us again; and it is like having an old friend back . . . The author has begun to externalize the elements of a complex personality in human figures that have a more complete existence than those of his previous stories." The only real cavilling came from Alvah Bessie in New Masses who leavened an opinion that *For Whom the Bell Tolls* was Hemingway's "finest achievement" with the warning: "But depth of understanding there is none, breadth of conception is heart-breakingly lacking; there is no searching, no probing, no grappling with the truths of human life that is more than superficial."

The sound you hear is that of sour grapes being pressed, for Bessie was only voicing the American left's chagrin that their version of the Spanish Civil War had been all but obliterated by the juggernaut of *For Whom the Bell Tolls*. As James Mellow put it so well: "It was certain that Hemingway's version . . . would be the version for the American public for years." To his eternal credit Hemingway, despite his devotion to the Loyalist cause, remained sufficiently objective to portray those whom the left-wing propagandists wanted to be presented only as chivalrous heroic martyrs as flawed humans capable of cowardice, treachery and arrogance: real people, in fact.

Compressing the dramatic events – personal, political and military – of four days and three nights in the life of Robert Jordan, sent into the Spanish hills to blow up a bridge and cut off advancing Nationalists, was a *tour de force* of which Hemingway was justly proud. During that short period Jordan meets and has an earth-moving night of passion with Maria, a 19-year old who had been raped after watching her parents being killed, and has to deal with the cowardly gypsy guerrilla leader and his woman, Pilar, who is beginning to assume leadership of the group. Fictional distrust, rivalry and double-dealing are interwoven with real civil war personalities and events to great effect, even if actual time-scales and chronologies became jumbled.

While Maria and Pilar remain two of the strongest female characters Hemingway ever wrote, time has been less kind to some of his stylistic tricks. Most irksome of all was his use of a strange Quakerish "thee" and "thou" English to characterize Spanish language dialogue.

As ever, Hemingway's old hang-ups and fantasies emerge. There are hints that Pilar and Maria have had, or are surreptitiously enjoying, a lesbian relationship. Jordan and Maria's sexual encounter bears more than a passing resemblance to Nick Adams and Katy's in *Summer People.* And when Robert Jordan fears that he may be charged with cowardice, memories of his own father's suicide (using a Smith and Wesson that once belonged to his U.S. Civil War veteran father!) include his observation: "He was just a coward and that was the worst luck any man could have. Because if he wasn't a coward he would have stood up to that woman and not let her bully him."

The hell-hounds of Oak Park were still on Hemingway's trail.

Only a matter of weeks after the publication of *For Whom the Bell Tolls,* Hemingway's marriage to Pauline Pfeiffer came to a legal end. Two weeks later, on November 21, he and Martha Gellhorn stood before a justice of the peace in Cheyenne, Wyoming, to declare their wedding vows. On hand to witness and photograph the ceremony for a two-part Life magazine photo essay was their friend Robert Capa. The first instalment – featuring shots of Hemingway and his new bride pheasant hunting in Sun Valley and dancing together – would be followed by a collection of Capa's Spanish Civil War photographs to accompany excerpts from *For Whom the Bell Tolls.*

Also present, but less than happy, was Martha's mother, Edna. She had arrived suddenly, intent on persuading her daughter to think again. Edna was not alone in considering the match ill-made. Whether it's apocryphal or not, Gertrude Stein was said to have pronounced that "a man who had married three women from St. Louis couldn't have learned much," while Scott Fitzgerald definitely told Maxwell Perkins: "It will be odd to think of Ernest married to a really attractive woman. I think the pattern will be somewhat different than with his Pygmalion-like creations."

Fitzgerald was right on the button for once. Martha had made it clear that she intended to carry on with her career and was not prepared to be sidelined into the role of little *hausfrau* and dinner party hostess. If Hemingway was happy to concede on that (and he had proved very supportive of her ambitions so far), the qualities which had first attracted him to Martha – her drive, undoubted talent and her ability to become "one of the boys" under enemy fire or at an all-night drinking party – were the very ones which would push him into an irrational jealousy that no marriage could hope to survive.

BELOW Celebrating with his new bride, Martha Gellhorn

Ernest and Martha on a trip to China reporting on the Chinese-Japanese war in 1941

On The Road Again

The two were, in fact, very different writers. Martha was, and would remain, a sharp-eyed observer and a gifted journalist capable of stripping away pretence and propaganda to inform her readers what the scores really were. Hemingway was a world-famous celebrity who, more often than not, used his fame to pronounce with assumed authority, generalizing with impunity and often settling for the well-rounded good-sounding phrase when a less adorned line would have served better.

It was so during their honeymoon, a long tour of a Far East embroiled in the Sino-Japanese War. Martha had been commissioned to file features for Collier's and Hemingway for P.M., a new liberal daily.

Martha's despatches expressed her horror at the dirt, deprivation, squalor and disease she saw everywhere in China, the ubiquity of opium dens and the abuse of young girls sold into prostitution. Hemingway's tended to grand overview: in Hong Kong (where they spent their first month) he blamed low morale on the enforced evacuation of British women who had been the colony's stabilizing element by keeping life on a formal basis; he reported on the sensations of drinking bird wine (with dead cuckoos in the bottle) and snake wine (serpants within rice wine).

After visiting the battle front at Canton they flew north to the wartime capital of China, Chungking, where they met and were photographed with Chiang Kai-shek, the Chinese political and military supremo whose wife acted as their interpreter. Later they would meet Zhou En-lai, theoretically charged with the task of liaising between

Communist leader Mao Tse-tung and Chiang but in fact living, fearful of Chiang, in secret locations. It was from Rangoon, Burma, that Hemingway would file seven dispatches to give an overview of the local situation, stressing Japan's urgent need for more oil and rubber if it was to win the war, the dangers implicit in the recently signed Russian-Japanese treaty, and the likelihood of Japanese aggression dragging the United States into a war it had so far refused to enter.

If Japan's attack on Pearl Harbor on December 7 took America by surprise, the overwhelming success of that venture – five battleships of the Pacific Fleet sunk or disabled along with 14 smaller vessels, 120 aircraft destroyed and more than 2,400 military and civilian personnel killed – did not surprise Hemingway and Martha. They passed through Hawaii during their Asian trek and had been troubled by the sight of so many warships packed into a site shared with numerous Japanese fishing boats, and of Hickham airfield filled with planes parked in neat, tight rows. Ducks had never sat so invitingly nor obligingly still for a hunter.

Hemingway fired off a series of furious letters. Army and navy commanders on Hawaii should be shot and Frank Knox, Secretary of the Navy, should have been fired immediately, he said. And to Charles Scribner he boomed: "Through our laziness, criminal carelessness, and blind arrogance we are fucked in this war as of the first day and we are going to have Christ's own bitter time to win it if, when, and ever."

Until then a vocal isolationist ("Never again should this country be put into a European war through mistaken idealism, through propaganda, through the desire to back our creditors . . . to make a going concern of a mismanaged one," he had written in 1935 predicting a European conflagration by 1938) Hemingway decided to do his bit. Cuba was a veritable hotbed of intrigue with Spanish Fascists, assorted Fifth Columnists, Loyalist veterans and German intelligence officers jostling for space and news. He could serve his country no better than by forming a counter-intelligence unit which, based in the guest house at Finca Vigía, could draw on information gathered by, among others, the many waiters and hotel staff he had befriended down the years.

Unbelievably, his plan – immediately called The Crook Factory – was given the green light by Spruille Braden, the U.S. Ambassador to Cuba, who appointed one of his staff, Robert Joyce, as liaison officer for the project. Equally bizarre was the approval Hemingway was given when, The Crook Factory not proving exciting enough, he decided to equip the Pilar with grenades and bazookas. Its role was to act as a one-ship task force dedicated to finding and destroying the German U-boats that patrolled the Caribbean for Allied warships and cargo craft.

Crewed variously by adoring locals who shared Papa's view that "We owe God a death" and, on occasions, volunteers as disparate as millionaire Winston Guest and Hemingway's sons, Patrick and Gregory, the *Pilar* was intended to act as an attractive target for surfaced subs. The idea was that the submarines would draw close enough for the *Pilar* crew to either open fire or hurl explosives into conning towers and hatches. It was a wild lunacy about which Colonel John Thomason – intelligence chief for Central America and the man who had helped Hemingway compile and edit *Men at War,* an anthology of war stories published in 1942 – expressed serious doubts, so earning himself the title "Doubting Thomason."

Martha, too, was a confirmed sceptic, openly and repeatedly voicing her well-founded suspicion that her husband's madcap scheme was merely an excuse for drunken boys' games, a device for circumventing petrol rationing so that fishing trips could continue and, worse, a defence for his tendency to let weeks pass without changing his clothes or bathing. Guerrilla leaders did not observe such bourgeois niceties and Papa Hemingway, now a self-proclaimed one-man army against the perfidious subaquatic enemy, was surely a guerrilla leader.

Martha's patience was stretched thinner and thinner as the Finca Vigía filled with a motley assortment of more or less permanent house guests and Hemingway's ever-growing collection of cats. "The place is so damned big it doesn't seem as if there were many cats until you see them all moving like a mass migration at feeding time," was his response to her weary protestations at the takeover staged by Tester, Dillinger, Tester's "wonder cat" kitten, Bates, Pony, Friendless (who learned to share Hemingway's milk and whiskey concoctions), Friendless's brother, Boissy D'Anglas (aka Boise, the name he would be known as in Hemingway's posthumously published *Islands in the Stream*) and Goodwill (who was named for America's goodwill ambassador, Nelson Rockefeller). The atmosphere grew tense at Crook Factory HQ when Hemingway returned from a trip to discover that Martha had, in his absence, had all the male cats neutered in a bid to end the rampant feline incest, which was producing blind and malformed offspring.

Offered an assignment by Collier's to report on the effects of German submarine activities on Caribbean islands including Puerto Rico, Haiti and Antigua, in August and September 1942 Martha was away from Cuba on a 30-foot sloop accompanied, as Hemingway explained disparagingly to Maxwell Perkins, ". . . by three faithful negro followers. I understand that if she is lost at sea, Colliers will pay double for her last

RIGHT Ernest and Martha sailing in the Caribbean

article. I expect they will also want me to write a Tribute to their intrepid correspondent." It was an unworthy jibe, but typical of many that Hemingway would make as Martha elected to undertake more assignments for which her talents were eminently suited.

As his wife's career and reputation blossomed, Hemingway's petulance grew, reaching a peak in late 1943 and early 1944 when she embarked on a dangerous journey which saw her reporting from England, North Africa and Italy. Later, when discussing the break-up of his marriage to Martha, Hemingway admitted: "What I wanted was a wife in bed at night, not somewhere having even higher adventures at so many thousand bucks the adventure."

Gregory Hemingway had clear memories of one particularly heated row when Martha returned home and had the temerity to plead that Hemingway abandon the Walter Mitty dreamworld she thought he occupied, to cut back on his drinking and get back to some writing. "I'll show you, you conceited bitch," he recalled his father shouting. "They'll be reading my stuff long after the worms have finished with you." It was a terrible thing to say, and while Hemingway was correct in predicting a kind of immortality for some of his own work, Martha's career and her reputation as a superb journalist would thrive until her death in February 1998 when obituarists acknowledged her as having been one of the most gifted and incisive writers on world affairs during the past 60 years.

With his private one-ship navy disbanded and the FBI given counter-espionage duties in the Caribbean, Hemingway was, in truth, at a loose end. While passing through Washingtom DC on her way back from Europe, Martha had been advised by Roald Dahl – then Assistant Air Attaché to the British Embassy – that the RAF would be delighted to have its activities written up for an American readership by someone as illustrious as Hemingway. He would certainly be allocated preferential air transportation to London and be set up as a person engaged in "priority war business" once there.

It was too good an offer to turn down and Hemingway was smart enough to know that Martha was right - he should get down to some writing. This was a chance to shine once more.

Despite the fact that Martha was Collier's accredited front-line correspondent (and was allowed only one journalist in that position) he offered his services to the magazine, an offer that was immediately accepted. When Martha asked if he could get her on to the RAF plane which was taking him to London, he said it was a men-only flight. She would learn later that Gertrude Lawrence and Beatrice Lillie, neither of whose femininity could be doubted, had been among the passengers who flew with Hemingway that day. It would be two weeks before Martha talked her way on to an air-freighter laden with dynamite and finally reached England again.

Martha arrived in London on May 28 to be informed that her husband had been seriously injured three days earlier in a dangerous car crash and was lying, reportedly, at death's door, in St. George's

Hospital. As Martha probably expected, it wasn't like that, of course. When she arrived at the hospital she found the patient, whose doctors had ordered complete rest and definitely no alcohol, lying on his bed surrounded by a number of visitors and the debris (which included bottles of whisky and champagne) of what clearly appeared to be a non-stop get-well party.

Since his arrival in London Hemingway had enjoyed a series of joyful reunions with old friends: Robert Capa was in town, working for Life magazine; Lewis Galantière had managed to flee Paris in 1939 and was ready to celebrate seeing his old friend again; and Hemingway's brother, Leicester, was also in town, working with William Saroyan and Irwin Shaw for a documentary film unit headed by Hollywood director George Stevens – a job Martha had fixed for him.

Set up in the relative luxury of the Dorchester Hotel, Hemingway had been having a fine old time in London and it was at the end of one such evening, as he was being driven back through the black-out to his hotel from Capa's Belgravia penthouse, that the car had crashed into a steel fire brigade water tanker. The driver, Dr Peter Gorer, and his wife were injured but Hemingway had come off the worst, suffering concussion and a deep scalp wound which resulted in 57 stitches. He also had extensive cuts and bruises to his knees.

In North Africa, where he was based with a U.S. military police unit, John Hemingway received a message that his father had, in fact, been killed and he subsequently went on a mighty drinking spree. It is not recorded whether or not hearing the truth the next day alleviated what was, by all accounts, a just as mighty hangover, but we can presume it helped somewhat.

If he had been expecting sympathy from Martha, Hemingway was in for a rude shock. Reunion led to a furious row during which Martha announced that she was fed up with him, his gigantic ego and his inability to act like an adult. Moving to another room in the Dorchester Hotel was the moment, she would later say, that she considered herself free of Hemingway.

In most respects Martha was free, for her husband had already – during the week or so he had been in London – met the woman he soon determined would become his next wife. There was only one small snag (although apparently not in their eyes): like Hemingway, Mary Welsh Monks too, was already married.

According to the most reliable accounts, the two first met at the White Tower Restaurant where Mary was dining with Irwin Shaw, her lover at the time. Petite, garrulous to the point of effusiveness and unafraid of stating her opinions, Mary was a feature writer for Time magazine and married to an Australian journalist, Noel Monks. Often separated by their assignments, their marriage had begun to drift. Hence the affair with Shaw and her immediate acceptance of a lunch invitation from the world-famous author who shamelessly gooseberried during her dinner with Shaw.

Mary's own version of events was that it was only after a few dates and before witnesses that Hemingway said grandly: "I don't know you, Mary. But I want to marry you." Pointing out the obvious snags (wife on his

side, husband on hers), she was told: "This war may keep us apart for a while . . . Just please remember that I want to marry you."

If Hemingway had one real regret it was that fame had made him too precious a cargo for the military authorities to allow him to go ashore during the D-Day landings on June 6, 1944. Fuming and frustrated, he was forced to watch events from the relative safety of a landing craft, his temper not helped by the later knowledge that Martha, who had stowed away on a hospital ship, had managed to steal ashore, so getting a real one-up on her husband.

Hemingway linked up as a non-combatant war correspondent with Colonel Charles "Buck" Lanham's 22nd Infantry Regiment – itself part of Major General Raymond O Barton's 4th U.S. Infantry Division, which spearheaded the Allied break-out from Normandy, helped capture Paris and held key positions during the Battle of the Bulge. Hemingway forged a deep instant friendship with the West Point graduate who would later (as a general) lead the troops who united with Soviet forces at the Moldau River, command occupation forces in post-war Austria and Czechoslovakia, and become General Eisenhower's chief spokesman at Supreme Headquarters, American Expeditionary Force (SHAEF).

Having all too often been confined to the frustrating role of a mere observer of warfare and his beliefs radically altered by what he'd witnessed during the Spanish civil war, Hemingway's period with U.S. forces between June 1944 and January 1945 gave him the opportunity to experience for himself precisely what it felt like to kill another human being.

Although he would claim to have despatched a number of Nazi troops on August 3 when, in the Normandy town of Villedieu-les-Poêles, he tossed grenades into a cellar where a number of the enemy were said to be hiding, Hemingway did not venture down the cellar steps to witness the carnage such an act would have caused, nor to substantiate his claim. But he definitely did kill some Germans on November 22 when he machine-gunned members of a force attacking Buck Lanham's HQ in the Hürtgenwald.

For the man who had drawn vivid analogies between war and the art of bullfighting but had so far contented himself with the vicarious thrill of big game hunting in Africa, the American West and the treacherous waters of the Gulf Stream, Hemingway could now boast of having lived through "the fear-purged, purging ecstasy of battle" and personally refute his own assertion (in the 1936 story *Wings Over Africa*) that: "The only people who loved war for long were profiteers, generals, staff officers and whores."

War was, he now believed, the ultimate competitive struggle, with the pleasure of absolute victory the most exhilarating of all. Recapturing France – and especially Paris – made him feel "the best I had ever felt . . . I had never known how winning can make you feel."

Lanham's memories of Hemingway, as recounted to New York Times correspondent CL Sulzberger, suggest that he had contracted the writer's inability to tell an exaggeration-free tale. Hemingway (who Lanham said

had "the heart of a lion" and was "entirely fearless") was depicted as wandering through the war with two canteens strapped to his belt – one containing gin, the other vermouth. At quiet moments Hemingway would produce a battered tin cup and suggest a Martini.

According to Jeffrey Meyers, this was not likely – Hemingway never carried a canteen of vermouth and did not drink heavily in combat situations. He may have been brave and fearless, but he was not an idiot.

That said, when a German farmhouse (immediately named Schloss Hemingstein) that Lanham was using as a field HQ came under artillery fire in September 1944, everyone dived for cover under the kitchen table or into a cellar. All except Hemingway that is. As shells rained down all around he sat alone, continuing to eat and drink, apparently unconcerned. When the bombardment ended and the others questioned his sanity, Hemingway airily explained that if you could hear a shell coming it would not harm you. War artist John Groth confessed that he couldn't decide whether Hemingway's action was valiant or stupid, intuitive or merely calculated to amaze his less courageous comrades. Whether either or neither, Groth, as many of the others, judged it both impressive and insane.

There was also a touch of madness in Hemingway's actions during the vicious fighting that took place around Rambouillet, some 30 kilometres south-west of Paris, in August. With the freedom of independent movement, which the allocation of a chauffeur-driven Jeep gave him, Hemingway patrolled ahead of the army and led a group of French partisans into the town, holding it for a day in which he established headquarters, raised the U.S. flag, took German prisoners and stacked his quarters with weapons. More importantly, the information he obtained about German defences along the road to Paris greatly aided General Jacques Leclerc's push on the capital, even if the general accepted that information disdainfully. He was forever after doomed to be referred to by Hemingway as "that jerk Leclerc."

That action, and Hemingway's refusal to wear the insignia which identified him as a correspondent, would result in his being summoned to SHAEF, then based in Nancy, to face charges that he had actively fought with the Resistance, had run an HQ complete with an adjutant and map-room and impeded the advance of official forces. Hemingway was on the horns of a very difficult dilemma. If he pleaded guilty, or was found guilty, he would lose his accreditation as a war correspondent and face instant repatriation and disgrace. If he lied he would be denying his own startling initiative and bravery. There was nothing to decide. Hemingway lied under oath, was acquitted and lived to join the final push into Germany, his war correspondent insignia firmly in place.

Before that there was reunion in Paris with Mary, who joined him in the suite he commandeered at The Ritz, and with Sylvia Beach and Adrienne Monnier who had survived the Nazi occupation of his favorite city. Shakespeare and Company had been forced to suspend operations during the war (books and other stock stored secretly in a fourth-floor apartment of their building), but was ready to resume business once something like normal life returned to Paris. At a literary party held at

LEFT AND BELOW The Parisian crowd welcomes in the Allied Forces to liberate France, August 25 1944

Beach's rue de l'Odéon apartment (and paid for by Life magazine)
Hemingway would hug Janet Flanner, read one of his poems and become
acquainted with Jean-Paul Sartre and Simone de Beauvoir, a couple he
later entertained grandly at The Ritz.

Although Gertrude Stein and Alice B. Toklas were still at the
countryside hidey-hole in which they'd spent most of the war, Pablo
Picasso was to be found at his studio on the rue des Grands-Augustins,
with Françoise Gilot, his new mistress and muse. Many bottles were
emptied in celebration and much talk was made of old friends who had
passed on since last they met – among them, Scott Fitzgerald (who had
died of accumulated good times in Hollywood in 1940), James Joyce and
Sherwood Anderson (both of whom had died in 1941, Joyce of
peritonitis following an operation in Zurich on a perforated ulcer, and
Anderson, also of peritonitis, in Panama).

Early in November Martha contacted Hemingway to suggest a divorce
(his affair with Mary having come to her attention) but he changed this
to an attempted reconciliation in an updating letter to Patrick. Eager to
convince his son that he had made the right choice in switching his
affection to Mary, Hemingway told Patrick he was ". . . going to get me
somebody who wants to stick around with me and let me be the writer of
the family." There were, however, a few last dark acts of the Hemingway
v Hemingway saga to be played out.

They took place during of the Battle of the Bulge, the massive
German counter-offensive against Allied forces in the Ardennes which
began on December 16. Dosed with sulfa pills to ward off a fever he'd
contracted while taking a break in Luxembourg, Hemingway was
dismayed by Martha's arrival at Buck Lanham's HQ at Rodenburg in
time for the Christmas and New Year celebrations. Her stay with the
regiment was, by all accounts, memorable if only for the amount of
malice which bristled between them and which climaxed with
Hemingway, armed with a mop for his lance and a bucket as his helmet,
laying siege to Martha's hotel room door until she ordered him away,
calling him a pathetic drunk.

The most telling encounter of all occurred when Buck Lanham took
them on a tour of command posts. Martha began needling Hemingway
in French from the back seat and Lanham, sitting beside her, watched as
Hemingway's neck grew redder and redder with rage. Suddenly a
German V2 flying bomb raced across the sky and Martha started
scribbling notes in her pad. "Remember this, Ernest," she said
vehemently, "that V2 story is mine!"

Hemingway and Martha would get together for one last time, in
March 1945 when he was passing through London on his way back
to America, the war in Europe all but over. Mary remained in Paris
on an assignment for Time magazine but had promised to meet him
in Cuba once her tour of duty was over. Martha was still living at the
Dorchester and laid up with influenza. Her mood was, however,
considerably lightened by Hemingway's statement that he had, at last,
agreed to a divorce.

They could both start getting on with the rest of their lives.

RIGHT A distinguished-looking Hemingway, circa 1944

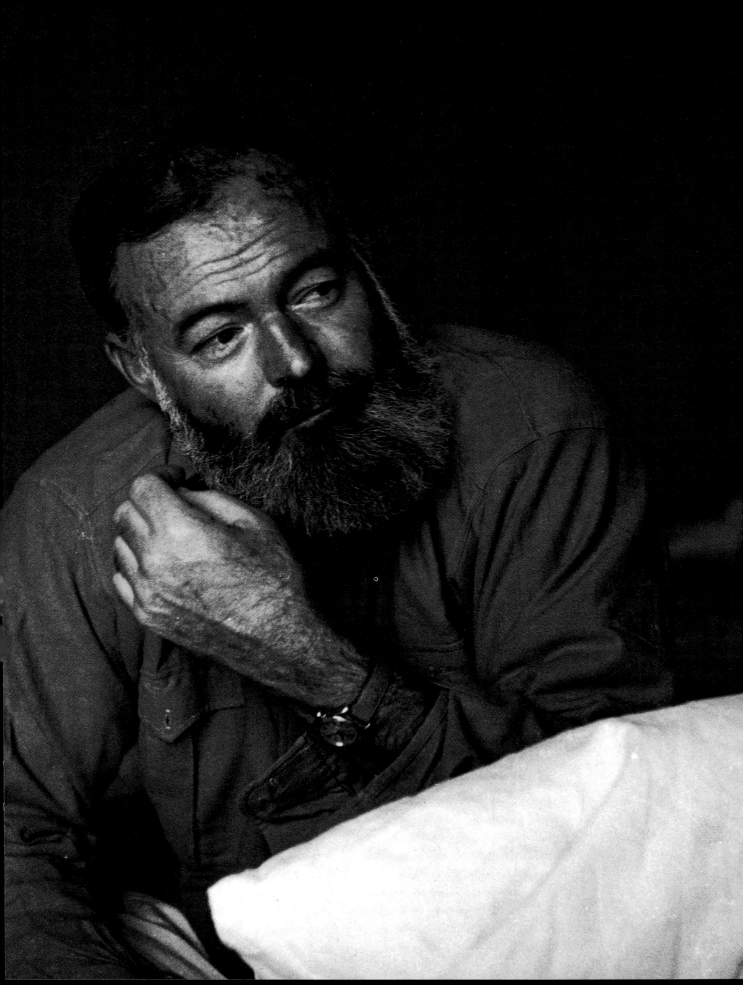

disaster

and triumph

(1945-1954)

Marriage to Mary

Hemingway returned to Cuba to find the Finca Vigía in a state of untended disarray after a hurricane, and his beloved cats in sore need of human care and affection. Both could be rectified in time and Hemingway had plenty of that. One of his first tasks was to begin repairs on the house and hire new staff, one of whom was a maid called Martha. He liked to order her about though the poor woman had no idea why she received such preferential treatment. There was also a fighting-cock stud to start. Hemingway's response to accusations of cruelty was perfunctory: "What the hell else does a fighting cock do?" he asked with impeccable logic.

Although the wheels of Cuba's legal system were turning in the task of processing his divorce from Martha on the grounds of her desertion (grounds which gave him possession of everything), they were doing so very slowly. It would not be until December 21, 1945 that the decree came through and he would have to wait until the following March until his marriage to Mary could take place.

If truth be told, Mary Welsh had serious reservations about becoming the fourth Mrs. Ernest Hemingway, having witnessed the least attractive aspects of his personality – the petulant rages, drunken boorishness and all – during the time they'd spent in Paris. During one argument following a drunken party, during which one of his 22nd Infantry Regiment buddies had thrown up in their Ritz Hotel bathroom, Mary had the temerity to suggest that his heroes were nothing but drunks and slobs. Hemingway slapped her and was shown the door, but only after Mary had justifiably responded with the taunts: "You poor coward. You poor, fat, feather-headed coward. You woman-hitter."

The life she settled for and into was, in many ways, idyllic. Hemingway's routine rarely altered, even when friends came calling or stayed. Mornings were for work, the rest of the day was for leisure, whether it be fishing, hunting or hanging out in favored bars with Cuban friends, drinking far too much and inevitably putting on weight. Time was also allocated to the creation of new, ever more potent cocktails, the pinnacle of which was reached with small ice pellets made of Gordon's gin with a dash of vermouth which produced an explosion of pure alcohol when tossed to the back of one's throat.

The work which occupied him for much of the first two years was, he told Maxwell Perkins, *The Garden of Eden,* a novel he eventually put aside to concentrate on what he called "my long sea novel." Also unfinished and not published until after his death when it was received with little enthusiasm, *Islands in the Stream* was actually three novels in one – *The Sea when Young, The Sea when Absent,* and *The Sea in Being.*

But they all came slowly and painfully, even more so when – in the summer of 1947 – Hemingway received word that Maxwell Perkins had died. An exhausted workaholic, Hemingway's most loyal acolyte, trusted friend and wisest counsellor contracted pleurisy and pneumonia before succumbing to a fatal heart attack in a hospital near his home in

ABOVE Wife number four – Mary Welsh, circa 1944

LEFT Hemingway at his writing desk in Cuba, 1945

Stamford, Connecticut. To Wallace Meyer, another Scribner editor, Hemingway wrote, later: "When Max died I did not think I could stand it. We understood each other so well that it was like having a part of yourself die."

Replying to Charles Scribner, who had written to express doubts about being able to fill Perkins' shoes, Hemingway advised him to "bury Max's ghost for keeps" and put him right about Scribner's star writers, each of whom had been Perkins' "babies." He did so in characteristically blunt fashion:

"Tom Wolfe was a one book boy and a glandular giant with the brains and guts of three mice," he advised Scribner, adding, "Scott was a rummy and a liar and dishonest about money with the in-bred talent of a dishonest and easily frightened angel." Whatever that meant. Hemingway was to be stunned, too, by the horrific death of Katy Dos Passos. Riding in her husband's car as he drove, she was catapulted through the windshield when Dos Passos, dazzled by sunlight, piled into a parked truck. The top of Katy's head had been sliced off and she died instantly. John Dos Passos survived but lost an eye, so condemning himself to be described, in later Hemingway outbursts, as "a one-eyed Portuguese bastard with Negro blood in his veins."

The two had, in fact, maintained a chilly estrangement since the end of the Spanish war when Dos Passos, disillusioned by rifts in the Spanish Communist Party, had all but completely withdrawn his once-fervent support for the Loyalists. Hemingway was outraged and remained so although he would bury the hatchet to join forces with Dos Passos, T.S. Eliot, Archibald MacLeish and others to campaign for the release from prison of Ezra Pound.

Arrested by American troops when they captured Italy, Pound's crime was to have broadcasted anti-semitic and anti-Allied propaganda throughout the war, his belief in Mussolini and fascism undiluted by time or reality, the latter of which became an increasing stranger to him. Like many fellow artists, Hemingway did not think that Pound, now clearly deranged but harmless, belonged in a prison.

The campaign to free him would continue until May 1958, at which time Hemingway sent him $1,000 to help with expenses. Deeply touched by his old friend's generosity, Pound did not cash the cheque but had it framed instead. He would die seven years later, having returned to Italy, and would be buried in Venice's municipal cemetery on the island of San Michele.

Frustrated by the slow advance of works supposedly in progress and self-chastised by the fact that his entire published output during the past five years had been a mere handful of articles for Collier's magazine, in the winter of 1948 Hemingway took Mary to Venice, desperately seeking inspiration and certainly hunting fresh memories of his past. It was there that the block which so afflicted him was briefly removed, the inspiration for his next novel coming from a serious though platonic infatuation he developed with an 18-year-old Italian girl, Adriana Ivancich.

The daughter of a wealthy Venezian family with a palazzo in the Calle di Rimedio, Adriana's path crossed with Hemingway's when they were both guests of Barone Nanyuki Franchetti at a duck-hunting weekend at Lasitana, some 70 km up the coast from Venice. It being December and the region inevitably cold, wet and windswept, he had remarked on her resilience. Later in the day he watched her trying to dry her long black hair by a fireside in a hunting lodge, realized that she did not have a comb, broke his in two and gave her one half.

From that moment Hemingway was smitten and Adriana became a constant companion, strictly chaperoned either by her understandably protective mother, an understanding Mary or by her 28-year-old brother, Gianfranco, a veteran of the Italian tanks corps and a former anti-fascist partisan. Strangely, while the intensity of Hemingway's infatuation with Adriana would drag on for close on six years, mostly in the form of fervent love letters and unwanted advice on the merits (or lack of them) of her various suitors, he would also "adopt" Gianfranco, invite him to live at the Finca Vigía and eventually lend him the money to buy his own home in Cuba.

According to Adriana, Hemingway did declare his love for her – during the spring of 1949, in Paris where she was studying art. She, Hemingway and Mary had taken lunch together after which she and Hemingway had walked to the Café Deux Magots for a drink and he had blurted out his declaration and his misery that he couldn't do anything about it. Startled, Adriana asked how Mary figured in all this and was told that while Mary had fine qualities, his was a marriage in which a crucial divergence of interests had already taken place. To her relief, for Adriana admitted to a rising sense of panic, Hemingway concluded his confession: "I would ask you to marry me, if I didn't know that you would say no."

Mary's attitude to Hemingway's mid-life crisis was remarkably sanguine, a word which could be applied in general to her perseverance throughout their life together. According to James Mellow, matters came to a head one evening at the Finca when Mary was helping Gianfranco with a U.S. visa application form (he was to accompany the Hemingways on a trip to Florida and the South before they all travelled to Italy) when Hemingway stormed into the room, picked up the typewriter she was using and hurled it to the floor. Later, in a dining room full of still-embarrassed guests, he pitched a glass of wine in her direction. It missed but smashed against the wall behind her.

Breaking the house rule which decreed his study an inviolable sanctuary in the mornings, Mary stormed in to let him know that whatever he did to try to make her leave, he was not going to succeed. "No matter what you say or do – short of killing me, which would be messy – I'm going to stay here and run your house and your Finca until the day when you come here, sober, in the morning, and tell me truthfully and straight that you want me to leave," she recalled in her memoirs, *How It Was.* He never did although his behavior and treatment of her often strayed well into realms any divorce trial judge and jury would have deemed both unreasonable and cruel.

There were to be many who wished that Hemingway's writer's block had restrained him from creating *Across the River and Into the Trees,* the

ABOVE An obviously content Hemingway in 1948, enjoying a relaxing meal

At the International Yacht Club in Havana during a Sailfish Tournament

novel inspired by his unrequited love for Adriana and also boasting one of her illustrations on its first-edition cover. Its title based on the last words of the American Civil War general, Thomas "Stonewall" Jackson, after the battle for Chancellorsville ("Let us cross over the river and rest under the shade of the trees"), it is widely acknowledged as Hemingway's worst novel.

Given that we know the title's origins, we can be sure that *Across the River* is going to be a novel about an old soldier who knows he is about to die. Hemingway's hero, Colonel Richard Cantwell, is not that old (he is actually 50, the same age as his creator) and dies, not of injuries incurred in battle, but of a heart attack in Venice after he has been involved in a torrid (and dreadfully written) affair with a beautiful 18-year-old contessa (with long black hair) called Renata. She is, impossibly, both innocent and sexually insatiable, the middle-aged man's ultimate fantasy.

Cantwell's recent career (the D-Day landings, Normandy campaign, recapture of Paris and the costly battle for Hürtgenwald) are described as adequately as any of Hemingway's inaccurate but exciting despatches for Collier's had been, but you don't need any clues to figure out the real-life inspiration for Cantwell's third wife, an ambitious self-serving former war correspondent from whom he is now separated.

Those looking for sub-texts need look no further than the origins of the name Renata, itself a clue to Cantwell/Hemingway's yearning for rejuvenation through an affair with a much younger woman. The Latin for re-birth is *renatus*, with the feminine being *renata*.

Across the River and Into the Trees managed to offend everybody, from Mary (who rightly believed that Maxwell Perkins would have told Hemingway to dump the many inconsequential mundanities littering the novel, re-think the dreadful mid-Victorian pornographic style in which the affair between Cantwell and Renata is conducted and described, and to tighten up the numerous chronological and geographical errors which occur), Adriana, her family and social set, to the critics invited to review the book when Scribner's published it in 1950.

Cyril Connolly, in the British Sunday Times, described it simply as "lamentable," while Maxwell Geismar, in the Saturday Review of Literature, decreed it not merely Hemingway's worst novel but "a synthesis of everything that is bad in his previous work." The San Francisco Chronicle reviewer, Joseph Henry Jackson, said he was awaiting the "longer, more important novel" Hemingway was rumored to be writing, and Philip Rahv – reporting for readers of Commentary magazine – warned them that it was not so much as "a parody by the author of his own manner – [but] a parody so biting that it virtually destroys . . . [the] legend of Hemingway that has now endured for nearly three decades."

Down, but definitely not out, Hemingway came back with an attempt to cast himself as a misunderstood experimental creative genius who had simply left the critics behind. "In writing," he told Harvey Breit during the course of an interview for the New York Times Book Review, "I have moved through arithmetic, through plane geometry and algebra, and now I am in calculus. If they don't understand that, to hell with them."

Despite this setback, Hemingway was suddenly hot property again, especially for those who wanted to gain his co-operation for what would be the first authorized biography. Carlos Baker, a distinguished professor of English at Princeton University, became involved in a lengthy and productive correspondence with Hemingway who, despite warning Baker that he wanted no biography written during his lifetime, began leaking him tantalising snippets of previously unknown information – his relationships with Hadley, Pauline and Martha included, and other women he'd slept with. After securing Baker's promise that his work was purely academic (a promise which Baker kept by deleting previously written biographical aspects of his study, *Hemingway: The Writer as Artist*) Hemingway opened up to the man from Princeton far more than he had any other writer.

When, for example, Grace Hemingway died in Memphis, Tennessee, on June 28, 1951, Hemingway expressed to Baker the second thoughts of the recently bereaved who are prepared to give the newly-departed some benefit of the doubt: "I have been thinking about how beautiful she was when she was young before everything went to hell in our family and about how happy we all were as children before it all broke up." This from a man who only months earlier had railed against Grace to Charles Scribner, describing her as "the old bitch" even as he wrote ordering her not to co-operate with a journalist preparing a biographical feature on him for McCall's magazine.

The fact is the journalist would probably have drawn a blank even if she had got an interview with Grace. Before being consigned to the tender ministrations of the Shelby County Hospital (a charity-funded institution and the nearest thing to a poorhouse then operating in Memphis), Grace had been living with Sunny, a daughter she no longer recognized and from whom she regularly ran away in a strange, childlike catch-me-if-you-can ritual. One part of her confused mind remained intact, however, for she could still play her own compositions on the piano from memory.

Hemingway did not, however, attend his mother's funeral but assisted with all of the arrangements by cable and telephone and organized for the church bell in San Francisco de Paula to toll throughout on the morning of her burial.

He was less forthcoming to Baker on the subject of Pauline when she died on October 1, in the same year, undergoing surgery for a tumor of the adrenal gland. In a letter sent shortly afterwards he mentioned her only as the mother of his two sons, and not by name. His reticence may have had something to do with his overwhelming sense of guilt – the night before she died, he and Pauline had spoken on the telephone and had a fierce exchange of words.

Writing to Charles Scribner only a day later Hemingway said: "The wave of remembering has finally broken over the jetty that I built to protect the open roadstead of my heart and I have the full sorrow of Pauline's death with all the harbor scum of what caused it. I loved her very much for many years and the hell with her faults."

The Old Man and The Sea

The writer who was to get closest to Hemingway during the last ten or so years of his life was Aaron Hotchner, a former USAAF officer who first met the author in 1948 when, as a writer for Cosmopolitan, he travelled to Cuba for an interview which was to be part of a feature, "The Future of Literature." The two had hit it off from the start and Hotchner became a trusted friend and drinking companion, not drawing on the often indiscreet revelations which spilled from Hemingway during late-night sessions until their originator was four years dead. Then his *Papa Hemingway* served to reinforce the larger-than-life legends which proliferated after Hemingway's dramatic suicide.

During 1951 the block which had eased enough to let him write *Across the River* shifted substantially, giving him the brainwave of shelving work on his sea trilogy (which was, in any case, still getting nowhere very slowly) and concentrating instead on developing the tale of the Cuban fisherman he'd heard from Carlos Gutierrez all those years ago. Originally intended to be only one element of *The Sea in Being,* it now worked as a stand-alone story and one which could – with some hard work – be turned into a novella.

Now entitled *The Old Man and the Sea,* Hemingway had shown or read early typewritten drafts to Carlos Baker, Aaron Hotchner and film producer Leland Hayward, all of whom had expressed themselves genuinely moved and excited both by the story itself and the quality of its telling. It was as if Hemingway had dug deep and found the master story-teller in himself once more.

This excitement was echoed at Scribner's when, in March 1952, Hemingway sent the uncorrected manuscript to Wallace Myer, now his editor. Meyer shared Hemingway's confidence which was expressed in the covering letter: "Publishing it now will get rid of the school of criticism that I am through as a writer . . . and claims I can write about nothing except myself and my own experiences."

As final correction work was done and publication day neared, Scribner's had nothing but the most exciting news for their man in Havana. In an unprecedented move, Life offered Hemingway $40,000 to publish the entire text of *The Old Man and the Sea* in its September 1 issue (which would sell an equally unprecedented 5,300,000 copies in two days) while the Book of the Month Club came up with a guarantee of $21,000 for its appearance as one of its dual selections in September. By publication, Scribner's were in receipt of 50,000 advance sales orders and would shift a further 3,000 copies a week during the six months *The Old Man and the Sea* stayed in the American best-seller lists. Later, Hemingway would sell the film rights (including his services as technical adviser) to Leland Hayward for a further $150,000. In all, that is close to $2 million in modern terms.

As gratifying as all that certainly was in financial terms (although he had no illusions about the grief that would eventually and inevitably come his way from the well-suited book-keepers in the Internal

RIGHT Ernest and Mary enjoying a corrida in Madrid

Revenue Service) Hemingway gained greater satisfaction from the ecstatic reception *The Old Man and the Sea* received from its reviewers. It was a complete vindication of his confidence in the story and in his re-found powers.

Typical of these was the British critic Cyril Connolly, whose Sunday Times review enthusiastically urged readers: "Get it at once, read it, wait a few days, read it again and you will find (except for an occasional loose 'now' or 'until') that no page of this beautiful master-work could have been done better or differently."

Likewise Orville Prescott, in the New York Times: "Here is a master technician once more at the top of his form, doing superbly what he can do better than anyone else."

To Hemingway's chagrin, however, many critics (including Carlos Baker) chose to read a Christian symbolism into the fact that Santiago, the fisherman, endures an ordeal which lasts three agonizing days and nights before his rescue and salvation, and stumbles and falls as he carries the mast of his skiff up the hill to his cabin. Hemingway, who said he held no brief for symbols ("If you have a message, call Western Union," he once told Mary), preferred the single most important message of the book to be the one he wrote to sum up Santiago's unquenchable spirit in the face of apparently overwhelming odds and reversals: "But man is not made for defeat. A man can be destroyed but not defeated."

The impact of *The Old Man and the Sea* on a broader level was remarkable. Sermons were preached with it as their theme, the Cuban régime of dictator Fulgencio Batistá (which Hemingway despised) awarded him a medal in the name of the professional marlin fishermen from Puerto Escondido to Bahía Honda, total strangers embraced him in the street, while his Italian translator was reputed to have burst into emotional tears as he worked.

It was on May 4, 1953 that Hemingway, on board the *Pilar,* received news that *The Old Man and the Sea* had won the Pulitzer Prize, an award he had thought he should have been given for *A Farewell to Arms* and/or *For Whom the Bell Tolls.* It really was a time for celebration and Hemingway planned to do it in style with a return to Africa and a reunion with his son, Patrick, who was now working a 2,000-acre farm in a remote part of Tanganyika with his wife, Henny.

Before that, however, there was the small matter of concluding negotiations with Leland Hayward for the movie rights and meeting Spencer Tracy, who would play Santiago once he had honored existing contractual commitments.

Coincidentally in Cuba at the same time was William Lowe, an editor from Look magazine, who offered Hemingway $15,000 towards the expenses of his safari along with another $10,000 for the rights to a 3500 word article which would be illustrated by the photographs of Earl Theisen. Before that Hemingway wanted to visit Spain again, beginning with the Pamplona feria in July. Greeted at Le Havre on June 30 by Gianfranco Ivancich, now a steamship line director, Hemingway and Mary motored into Spain in a Lancia owned and chauffeured by a young funeral director friend of Gianfranco's.

Pamplona, now a truly international tourist attraction thanks in part to Hemingway's publicizing of its charms, had no available place of rest even for such a luminary as el Papa so they (in a party now including Juanito Quintana, whose beloved Hotel Perla had been destroyed during the civil war) were forced to find rooms in Lecumberri, a village some 40 km away. Although the first corrida had been a disappointment, the second day brought satisfaction in the performance of the dashing young Antonio Ordonez, the son of Nino de la Palma, Hemingway's inspiration for the matador Pedro Romero in *The Sun Also Rises*.

On to Madrid and a return to the Hotel Florida, scene of the younger Hemingway's civil war nights with Martha Gellhorn. Although Mary did not take to the city's arid climate or the day-and-night clatter of electric trams as they trundled past the hotel, she did share with pleasure the hour each morning Hemingway insisted they spent viewing the paintings housed in the Prado, where he was particularly taken by Hieronymous Bosch's fantastical tryptich, *The Garden of Earthly Delights*. After touring more of his old Spanish haunts they made for France and the ship which was to take them from Marseilles to Mombassa.

It was raining when they arrived at the Kenyan port to be met by Philip Percival who, 20 years older since he and Hemingway last met, had appropriately thickened waist and thinned hair. Photographer Earl Theisen and Mario "Mayito" Menocal, a Cuban friend, were to rendezvous with them at Percival's farm near Nairobi. Storm clouds were looming however and a safari which began promisingly soon deteriorated into farce, and worse.

Now drinking heavily and unable to match Menocal's marksmanship, Hemingway's behavior began to veer between morose and manic. He took up with a young Wakamba girl, re-named her Debba and spoke of her as his fiancee. Then, when Mary was away in Nairobi on a Christmas present-buying trip, Hemingway shot a leopard and began a drunken celebration which culminated in him bringing a group of local girls to the camp for a party during which Mary's camp-bed was broken.

Mary's sanguinity reserves appear to have been bottomless during all this, for Hemingway was able to inform Harvey Breit, in a letter he wrote to the man from the New York Times, that she "just stays the hell away from it and is understanding and wonderful." As her reward, Hemingway arranged for what he hoped would be the trip of a lifetime but would, in fact, prove to be a nightmare from which he would never really recover.

On January 21, 1954 he and Mary took off aboard a chartered Cessna 180 piloted by Roy Marsh, a bush pilot who had previously taken them on local excursions. This time their flight was to be over the even wilder country found in the eastern Congo with stops in Bukavu, which boasted a good hotel. They ran into trouble almost immediately when generator problems forced Marsh to set down in Mwanza for repairs, although he was able to get them to Bukavu. Day 2 saw them fly north over active volcanoes and on to Rwanda's legendary Mountains of the Moon which were, unfortunately, shrouded in impenetrable clouds.

Their third flight took them from the Ugandan city of Entebbe along the western shore of Lake Albert until they reached Murchison Falls,

BELOW Grimacing at the mention of his two famous air-crashes – Hemingway in Genoa

Marsh circling the spectacular cataracts which tumble into the gorge below while Mary shot a couple of rolls of film. It was as they were returning to Entebbe that the Cessna was forced to dive in order to avoid a flock of birds. Down to tree-top level, the plane snagged a telegraph wire which disabled its rudder. Marsh managed to crash-land his craft among heavy brush. Thankfully, the Cessna did not catch fire and its three occupants scrambled clear of the wreckage, Mary already suffering agonies from the two ribs which had broken in the crash.

With the plane's radio smashed and evening dusk beginning to fall the trio salvaged a bottle of malt whiskey as a small comfort for the night which lay ahead. As the river bank near which the Cessna had come down was home to a number of interested crocodiles, they set up a rough and ready camp some distance away.

Morning brought the miraculous sight of the *Murchison,* the steam launch which had starred as the eponymous heroine of John Huston's movie *The African Queen.* Chartered by a British surgeon, Dr McAdam, for his family, the *Murchison* readily turned about to take them back to the relative civilization of Butiaba, where a Captain Reggie Cartwright was waiting to tell Hemingway that he had already been declared dead, a host of pressmen was even now assembling in Entebbe to file follow-up stories and search planes were still vainly trying to find the crash site.

Cartwright owned a De Havilland Rapide and suggested he fly them to Entebbe. Even though night was beginning to fall and the wisest course would have been to rest up in Butiaba before going on, Hemingway decided to accept Cartwright's offer. It was a bad call. In near darkness and on a runway no better than a plowed strip, the bi-plane crashed on take-off, bursting into flames.

While Mary, Walsh and Cartwright managed to smash their way out, Hemingway found his door blocked by a jagged shard of metal. Using his head and an already dislocated shoulder as battering rams he managed to escape the worst of the fire, but not without suffering a severe

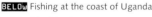
BELOW Fishing at the coast of Uganda

concussion. If that was not bad enough, his scalp was bleeding heavily and cerebral fluid was trickling down behind his left ear.

The nearest reliable doctor being some way away in Nasindi, the stricken party decided to drive there and found a telegraph office whose operator refused to contact Entebbe, it being a Sunday and he being bound by red-tape restrictions concerning the Lord's day. At the Railway Hotel the last serving of dinner had already ended so they had only sandwiches. The next morning the "reliable" doctor merely bandaged Hemingway's still-bleeding and suppurating wounds, dabbed iodine on the deep gashes which covered his legs and did likewise for Mary's cuts.

In Entebbe the press pack met them (and duly got interviews with the newly risen Papa) and the sight of newspapers carrying very premature obituaries. When they finally got back to the comfort of Nairobi's New Stanley Hotel, Hemingway had the unique opportunity of reading what his peers really thought of him and his life's work. He was, in the main, pleased with the judgements passed although puzzled at a common strand which conjectured that he had flirted with death all his life.

"Can one imagine that if a man sought death all his life he could not have found her before the age of 54?" Hemingway pondered in the two-part feature, "The Christmas-Gift," Look published later that year. It is revealing that while Death is almost universally depicted as a masculine figure, Hemingway chose to portray it as female.

Although Hemingway expressed himself fit enough to make a long-planned fishing trip with Percival, Patrick and Henny at the end of February, Mary was concerned that he was not in fact recovering well or quickly. Basing themselves at Shimoni, near Mombassa, the party was subjected to ever wilder mood swings from Hemingway, obviously in pain and uncharacteristically reluctant to do much fishing. During one of his outbursts Hemingway reduced Henny to tears as he berated Patrick for not preparing bait for an expedition. Patrick snapped and ordered his and Henny's equipment to be loaded into their Land-Rover.

It would not be until they reached Venice, some three months after the air crashes, that the full extent and severity of Hemingway's injuries were diagnosed properly. According to Mary he had suffered two cracked and impacted spinal disks, ruptures to his liver, spleen and one kidney, temporary loss of vision to one eye, almost complete loss of hearing to his left ear, paralysis of the sphincter, his skull seriously fractured, both his arm and right shoulder dislocated and first degree burns to his face, arms and head. Death, whether male or female, had indeed come close.

Aaron Hotchner was appalled by his first sight of Hemingway when he visited Cuba a while after the Hemingways arrived home. "What was shocking to me now was how he had aged in the intervening five months," he wrote in *Papa Hemingway*. "What there was of his hair (most of it had been burned off) had turned from brindle to white, as had his beard; and he appeared to have diminished somewhat – I don't mean physically diminished, but some of the aura of massiveness seemed to have gone out of him."

BELOW Pursuing his favourite sports – shooting on the river

The Nobel Prize

If 1954 was a year which had begun badly, it was to end triumphantly with news that Ernest Miller Hemingway had finally won the Nobel Prize for Literature he had coveted for so long. That news came in the form of a phone call from United Press in the morning of October 28, followed shortly after by an invasion of well-wishers, reporters and photographers into the grounds of the Finca Vigía.

After waking Mary to tell her, "My kitten, my kitten, I've got that thing!," he telephoned Buck Lanham, again saying he'd got "that thing." It was a "thing" which had already been awarded to Sinclair Lewis and William Faulkner, both of whom Hemingway had little respect for either as writers or men, and one which he suggested – with rare generosity – in a telephone interview with Harvey Breit should have gone to Bernhard Berenson, Isak Dinesen or Carl Sandburg.

If he was content with the prize itself, Hemingway was less pleased with the official citation issued by the Nobel Committee, which described him as having come through an early "brutal, cynical and callous" phase to emerge with a "powerful, style-making mastery of the art of modern narration." As Anthony Burgess has commented, it was an inept summary of Hemingway's literary career while "style-making" (which means nothing) sounds like "a cybernetic rendering of a Swedish word that means something different."

Unfit to travel to Stockholm for the presentation ceremony (and in any case a man with a dread of public speaking) Hemingway persuaded John Cabot, U.S. ambassador to Sweden, to deliver his acceptance speech. It was well-considered and gracious and said in part:

"Writing, at its best, is a lonely life. Organizations for writers palliate the writer's loneliness but I doubt if they improve his writing. He grows in public stature as he sheds his loneliness and often his work deteriorates. For he does his work alone and if he is a good enough writer he must face eternity, or the lack of it, each day.

"For a true writer each book should be a new beginning where he tries again for something that is beyond attainment. He should always try for something that has never been done or that others have tried and failed. Then sometimes, with great luck, he will succeed. How simple the writing of literature would be if it were only necessary to write in another way what has been well written. It is because we have had such great writers in the past that a writer is driven far out past where he can go, out to where no one can help him. I have spoken too long for a writer. A writer should write what he has to say and not speak it. Again I thank you."

Privately, Hemingway told friends: "No son of a bitch that ever won the Nobel Prize ever wrote anything worth reading afterwards." Sadly, in his case, this was to be only too true.

RIGHT A triumphant Hemingway at home in Cuba, admiring his Nobel Prize for Literature

the morning (1954–1961)

A Farewell to Cuba

The aftermath of winning the Nobel Prize included an ordeal by visitor as the Finca Vigía became the place to be for a horde of celebrities, many of whom Hemingway would not normally have given the time of day, let alone the hospitality of his beloved retreat. Vanity, however, prevailed.

If a part of him was flattered by this explosion of interest and another satisfied by the praise which such visitors rained on him, the fruits of success often bore the bitter taste of sycophancy and insincerity. Then there were the busloads of rubbernecking tourists, the avid ever-inventive fans and other loopies who managed to reach the front door, the eager young writers seeking pearls of wisdom, and the pedantic academics who wanted him to help them deconstruct his work to confirm their own highflown theories.

There was no escape to be found in work for the inspiration which had resulted in *The Old Man and The Sea* had proved a false mistress, abandoning him once more. With Mary as his typist he returned fitfully to the *Island in the Stream* trilogy and *The Garden of Eden*. Worse even than the constant interruptions of guests and interlopers was the fact that Cuba itself was changing, the Batistá régime now under almost constant attack from rebels and revolutionaries, its frightened police and military responding with brutish arrogance. It was unwise to speak out, so Hemingway kept his own counsel even when a government patrol – ostensibly hunting a rebel fugitive – entered the Finca's grounds and killed one of his dogs. Time was, some local official would have felt the edge of Papa's tongue.

For close on two years this sorry state of affairs meandered on, Hemingway's growing unhappiness only salved by the ever-growing amounts of alcohol he was consuming. That diet inevitably wreaked its havoc on his body so that, by the beginning of 1957, his doctors were forced to advise him to cut back (it was useless to tell him to cut out) on his drinking, for his blood pressure and cholesterol counts were dangerously high and his liver was in danger of collapse. They also warned him off the ingestion of fatty foods and love-making.

Taking himself to Europe during the winter of 1956–57, Hemingway was resident at the Ritz, in Paris, when someone mentioned the existence of two old trunks which were languishing in the hotel's cellars since 1928. Intrigued, for he had little memory of them, Hemingway was thrilled to discover that they were full of handwritten notes, aborted first drafts of fiction and reportage. The good old days in note form.

Informing Scribner's that he was now working on his memoirs, Hemingway set to work on what would eventually emerge, after his death, as *A Moveable Feast,* a fascinating (though often scurrilous and always self-serving) series of vignettes in which he attempted to recapture some of the heady innocent excitement of those far-off days, re-appraise his contemporaries and – secure in the knowledge that one cannot libel the dead – deliver some broadsides that he knew would not be answered from the grave.

LEFT An increasingly weary Hemingway talks to a journalist in Peru, where he had flown down for the filming of *The Old Man and the Sea.*

PREVIOUS PAGE The Hemingway family and friends at his graveside on the day of his funeral, 1961

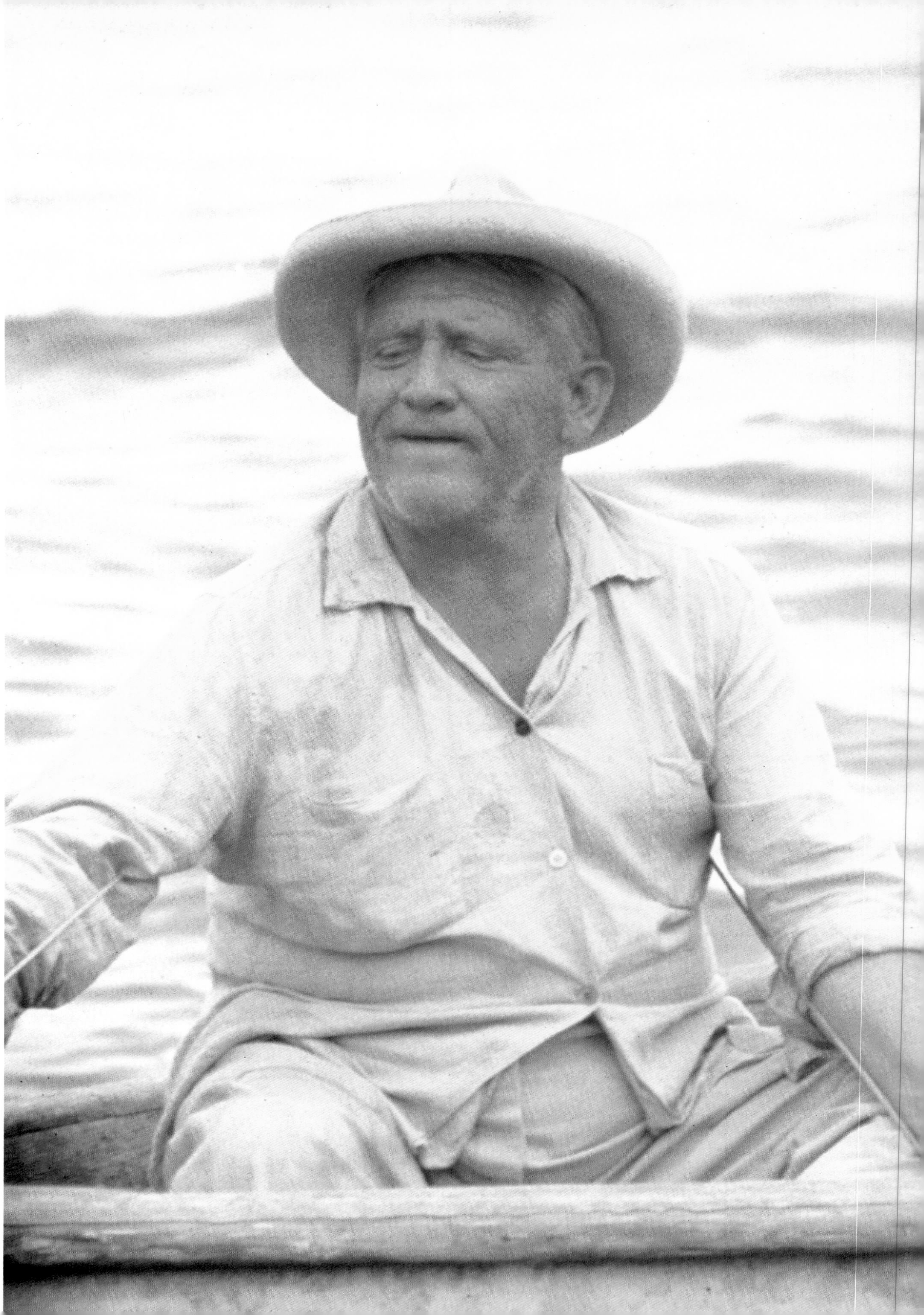

Thus, he could humiliate Gertrude Stein (who had moved on to the great salon in the sky in 1946, but not before reportedly asking Alice Toklas, "What is the answer?" and, when "Miss Tocraz" volunteered no reply, added: "In that case, what is the question?") with an account of her embarrassing lesbian surrender to Toklas after a row he'd witnessed, depict Dos Passos as a mere sycophantic acolyte, blame the blameless Gerald and Sara Murphy for wrecking his marriage to Hadley and despoiling his talent with the allure of their unlimited wealth, and repeat his often-repeated theory that the root of Scott Fitzgerald's insecurity lay in his concern about the size of his penis.

As James Mellow has remarked, it is frustrating to think what a memoir of those years – when he was a leading player on a stage peopled by some of "the most extraordinary writers, artists, playwrights, composers, architects, publishers, publicists, scholars and critics" who had redefined and re-shaped the culture of their time in Paris, Berlin, Moscow, London and New York – could have been at the hand of a Hemingway at the peak of his powers. Sadly, *A Moveable Feast* was written by a sick man of fast-waning skills intent, most of all, on confirming the cult of celebrity which had sprung up around him and the legends he himself had created along the way.

There was diversion of sorts in the filming of Cuban sequences for *The Old Man and The Sea* when he was obliged to provide the services as technical adviser he'd contracted for, but his experiences and impressions of that were very mixed.

He was not, for instance, overly impressed by Spencer Tracy's appearance ("very fat for a fisherman," he commented of an actor who,

stricken with self-doubt, was drinking heavily), the temper tantrums of cast and crew, nor the large glass-eyed model marlin built for some sequences ("There is nothing a rubber fish cannot fix," he told Gianfranco Ivancich wryly in a letter). He would write an exasperated note to Gary Cooper once local filming was completed: "Coops, after *The Old Man and The Sea* is finished I will not ever have anything to do with pictures again so Help Me God. God is Capitalized."

Aware that the growing successes of Fidel Castro's revolutionary army (formed from the small band of guerrillas which survived a disastrous landing from the rustbucket Granma in December 1956) spelled the imminent end of the Batistá régime and, possibly, his residency visa, Hemingway purchased a large house in Ketchum, Idaho, in good shooting and fishing country, near the banks of the Big River, surrounded by cottonwoods and aspen and with spectacular views of the mountains. Just in case.

He was in Ketchum on New Year's Day, 1959, when the New York Times called to ask for his opinion on news that Fulgencio Batistá had fled Cuba and a column of Fidel Castro's army led by Che Guevara had reportedly taken the capital. Hemingway spontaneously pronounced himself "delighted," only to be warned by Mary that he ought to be more circumspect – no one knew for sure if Castro's régime would be any less brutal or corrupt than Batistá's. Dutifully, Hemingway called the Times newsdesk and asked them to change his opinion to "hopeful."

His concerns for the Finca and his invaluable collection of books and paintings were mollified by a call from Jaime Bofils, a Castro government official who'd been charged with protecting the Hemingway home and estate. Much later, and after he'd returned to Cuba in 1960 to host a marlin fishing contest which *el commandante* duly won, the Finca Vigía and much of its treasures would be seized by a régime which the United States was now treating as a dangerous wild dog, having failed to muzzle it in the April 1961 Bay of Pigs fiasco. By then Hemingway was a broken man who needed nothing to feed his paranoia.

A great number of Hemingway's personal papers, including discarded draft manuscripts, had also been deposited for safety in a Havana bank vault. These would not be lost after the revolution, however. According to Mary, in a letter she wrote to author Stanley Booth in 1963 thanking him for an appreciation of Hemingway he'd written for Phoenix magazine, in July 1961 she had returned to Cuba and retrieved everything thought lost.

Invited by a wealthy friend, Nathan "Bill" Davis, to be his guest that summer at a projected *mano a mano* encounter between Luis Miguel Domínguín and his brother-in-law rival, Antonio Ordonez, Hemingway made plans to celebrate his sixtieth birthday in Spain. Life pitched in with a tempting commission for a 10,000-word feature to seal the idea. He, Mary, Gianfranco, Aaron Hotchner, Juanito Quintana, assorted wives, lovers and Bill Davis's own sizeable entourage embarked on a trek during which Hemingway – as befitted his status as Nobel laureate and author of *Death in the Afternoon,* the longest love poem to a country, its people and its major secular ritual – was treated like a visiting deity.

LEFT Papa Hemingway and Mary, looking relaxed and happy at a bullfight in Spain

Buck Lanham arrived in time to be a guest at the birthday party Mary had spent weeks organizing at La Consula, Bill Davis's spacious villa in Malaga. It really was spectacular, complete with flamenco dancers, guitar players, fireworks and a shooting gallery in which Antonio Ordonez proved his courage by allowing a very drunk Hemingway to blast shots at the lighted cigarettes the matador held between what must have been very tightly clenched teeth.

Depression and Decline

Lanham was to witness Hemingway's mental deterioration – some believed encroaching dementia – shortly before that, at another celebration held at the Hotel Miramar. Moved to tears when Buck presented him with an inscribed copy of a history of the 22nd Infantry Regiment, Hemingway later dissolved into a rage when the warrior hero grasped his shoulder affectionately and accidentally brushed the back of his head.

No one, Hemingway screamed, was permitted to touch his head. Lanham stalked out, furious, only to be followed by a weeping and apologetic author who explained that he was sensitive about having to comb his hair forwards in order to hide his fast-spreading bald patch. Lanham was placated but departed unsettled by Hemingway's now incessant use of obscenities and what he perceived as an "unhealthy nostalgia for his young manhood."

Proof of Hemingway's paranoia, especially in matters financial (which were nonsensical for a man already rich and receiving close on $100,000 a year in royalties), was his post-party accusation that Mary had lavished too much of "his" money on the event. She was able to prove that she had, in fact, used her fees from a feature she'd written for Sports Illustrated to pay for the celebration, but got her revenge by writing from Cuba (where she'd gone ahead to prepare the Finca Vigía for a visit by Antonio Ordonez and his wife, who were also due to spend time in Ketchum) suggesting that as he obviously did not trust her, nor had any real use of her, she would find herself an apartment in New York.

She received a grovelling telegram of apology in return – and a diamond pin when Hemingway and their guests arrived in Cuba. Ordonez turned out to be less interested in experiencing the thrills of fishing than perfecting his suntan and would be no less excited by the prospect of duck-hunting in Idaho. Shortly after they all arrived in Ketchum, Ordonez received an "unexpected" call to say that his sister needed him in Mexico – she was breaking up with her husband.

Hemingway battled on with the Life feature which continued to grow well past its nominated 10,000 words. By June 1960 it had swelled to 120,000 words, none of which Hemingway appeared willing, or capable, of editing. Plans for Scribner's to publish what Hemingway called "the Paris book" (A Moveable Feast) were shelved and Aaron Hotchner was recruited to help trim the Life article (now called "The Dangerous Summer") to a more manageable 70,000 words, which the magazine

accepted – they would edit it further themselves – and paid $100,000 for, $10,000 of which was to cover Spanish language rights.

Of equal concern throughout that period was Hemingway's growing conviction that the FBI were out to get him. He was correct to a degree, for J. Edgar Hoover's charcoal "suits" had possessed a file marked "Hemingway, E.M." since the wild and wacky days of The Crook Factory. What tipped the scales against Hemingway was his tacit approval of Castro's Cuban revolution, his return to Cuba in the spring of 1960 and the widespread publication of photographs capturing the moment he presented a beaming Castro with the championship cup.

But Hemingway became a conspiracy theorist of the highest order. When he noticed lights burning late at night in a local bank, for instance, no amount of rational explanations (such as cleaners at work) could dissuade him from the conviction that it was the FBI "trying to get something" on him. It was to get worse.

Convinced that he needed to go back to Spain to supervize photography for "The Dangerous Summer" and accompany Ordonez around the circuit, Hemingway left Mary in New York on August 4, flying TWA to Madrid. Four days later she heard from Hotchner that news broadcasts were reporting that her husband had collapsed and died in Malaga. Her frantic enquiries ended with a cable from Hemingway telling her he was fine, but his follow-up letters were ominously dark in

tone, most especially one in which he wrote: "I wish you were here to look after me and help me out and keep from cracking up."

He was not pleased when she sent him copies of the first installment of "The Dangerous Summer" which, she reported, was a huge hit in New York, with Scribner's windows full of his collected works and blow-ups of the Life pages. He hated the portrait of him Life used on the cover and expressed himself ". . . ashamed and sick to have done such a job." He railed against the selected bullfight pictures, saying they were "not fair" to Ordonez or Dominguín who would surely consider him "an all-time fool and a double-crosser."

At Bill Davis's home, La Consula, Hemingway kept to his bed for days, remained silent when he did get up and told Hotchner that Davis was trying to kill him in a car wreck. And when it came time for him to return home, Hemingway was convinced that the airline would not allow him to travel with the luggage he'd accumulated. Hotchner had to get a signed statement from TWA before Hemingway would agree to board the flight.

Mary was waiting for him at Idlewild Airport, New York, but any thoughts she had that he wasn't as bad as she'd feared ended when he refused to leave the apartment. "Somebody waiting out there," he told

ABOVE Hemingway setting out on a morning of hunting

her and, when she told him to stop acting like some damned fugitive, slumped into silent brooding. She cajoled him into taking the train back to Ketchum, via Chicago, but the journey turned bizarre when Hemingway noticed two men in coats passing by at the Shoshone station. "They're tailing me out here already," he told her firmly.

In Ketchum his financial affairs became the subject for a manic distrust which was not assuaged when Mary arranged for the vice-president of Morgan Guranty Trust in New York to call with a reading of the balances of his many accounts. "He's covering up something," Hemingway said flatly. In fact, he would leave an estate valued at more than $4 million.

It would not be until November 1960, and then only at the insistence of Hotchner and Hemingway's physician, Dr George Saviers, that Mary agreed to explore the option of psychiatric treatment. Hemingway, however, obdurately refused to become a patient at the Menninger Clinic, a leading psychiatric facility ("They'll say I'm losing my marbles!") but on November 30 did allow himself to be secretly treated by the Mayo Clinic in Rochester, Minnesota, registering at St. Mary's Hospital as George Saviers and in the guise of a man being treated merely for high blood pressure. Mary checked into a nearby hotel, registering herself as Mrs. Saviers.

Initial medical reports not only confirmed that Hemingway did, in fact, have high blood pressure and cholesterol counts but suggested that he was suffering from a form of diabetes mellitus. One of the medical team also suspected that Hemingway had hemochromatosis, a congenital metabolic disorder which involves an accumulation of iron in the body system which adversely, and irreversibly, affects the heart, liver and other vital organs. Deciding to take him off the reserpine he'd been prescribed for his blood pressure (its side-effects included depression), the Mayo team recommended that he be given electric shock therapy twice a week for a number of weeks.

News of Hemingway's incarceration did not break until six weeks later and his sagging spirits were lifted by the flood of get-well letters, cards and telegrams, one from the newly-elected president, John F Kennedy, inviting him to Washington for the inauguration ceremony. Hemingway declined on health grounds and watched it with Mary on television.

During his first stay in hospital Hemingway wrote a sad, strange letter addressed "To whom it may concern," exonerating Mary from any charges of illegal conduct or misdeeds relating to either his finances or registering him under an alias. Released from the Mayo's care on January 22, he and Mary returned home to Ketchum where his mornings were spent trying to work on *A Moveable Feast* and his afternoons, more often than not, walking along Route 93. Invited to contribute to a presentation volume for Kennedy, Hemingway spent hours vainly battling against the block, eventually breaking down, weeping, and telling Dr Saviers that he couldn't write any more and the shock treatment had destroyed his ability.

At night he took to standing at Mary's bedroom door, lambasting her for spending too much on groceries and complaining that she was not concerned about "the dangers" of living in Idaho. One morning Mary found him standing in the hall with a shotgun in his hands. Talking him down, she was aided by George Saviers, who had arrived shortly after on a routine housecall. It was he who persuaded Hemingway to go with him to the nearby Sun Valley Hospital prior to returning to the Mayo. Allowed to go home and collect a few personal effects, Hemingway made a beeline for the basement stairs and his gun collection. There was a scuffle before his friend, Don Anderson, was able to wrestle a weapon from his grasp. The next day, en route for Rochester and during a refuelling stop in Rapid City, Hemingway strode purposefully across the runway tarmac towards the revolving propeller of another aircraft. Spotting him in time, the pilot cut his engine.

Assigned to a closed barred-window ward at St. Mary's, Hemingway submitted himself once more to shock treatment but accused Mary of "setting things up" so that he would be sent to jail. A few weeks later, to her astonishment, Mary received a call to say that her husband was feeling much better and his sexual drive had returned. Racing to Rochester, she and Hemingway spent a surreal afternoon together on his narrow bed as fellow inmates ("hollowed-eyed men looking for something we could not give them," as she noted, later) shuffled by.

Suicide

Two days later Mary received word that the hospital was prepared to release Hemingway. He had managed to fool his doctors, into letting him go home, even if Mary herself was not fooled.

Back in Ketchum, Hemingway's initial joy at being home and seeing his old sights and friends again soon began to wane and it seemed that not even the verdant splendor of a relaxing Idaho summer could raise him from the morose lethargy which overtook him. He sat day after day in the corner, saying nothing to anyone who came calling.

On Saturday, July 1, Hemingway and Mary went with a friend to a local restaurant. During the meal, which passed pleasantly enough, Hemingway noticed two men sitting at another table and asked who they were. Told that they were salesmen, Hemingway shook his head gravely and replied: "They're FBI."

Back home, as they undressed for bed, Mary sang him one of his favorite airs, "Tutti mi chiamano bionda," and Hemingway joined in. They retired for the night – he to the back bedroom, she to the front.

On the morning of July 2, 1961, at around dawn, lying in her bed, Mary heard the dull, thudding sound which signalled the end of Ernest Hemingway's despair and his life.

Among the vast avalanche of tributes which were made to Ernest Hemingway in the following days was one Hemingway himself would have undoubtedly cherished above all. In Madrid, Antonio Ordonez dedicated a bull to el Papa, and was duly awarded both ears and the tail.

RIGHT A grand commemorative monument to a larger than life character – this bust of Hemingway stands in Cojimar, Cuba

ERNEST
HEMINGWAY
1898 — 1961

Publishing Director: Laura Bamford
Executive Editor: Mike Evans
Editor: Humaira Husain
Creative Director: Keith Martin
Senior Designer: Geoff Borin
Design: Martin Topping
Production Controller: Claire Smedley
Picture Research: Zoë Holtermann

First published in the U.S. in 1999 by
Chicago Review Press, **Incorporated**, 814 North Franklin Street,
Chicago, Illinois 60610.

First published in the UK in 1998 by **Hamlyn**, an imprint of
Octopus Publishing Group Ltd, Michelin House, 81 Fulham Road,
London SW3 6RB.

©1998 Octopus Publishing Group Ltd

ISBN 1-55652-339-4

Printed and bound in China

The publishers wish to thank the following individuals and organizations
for their kind permission to reproduce the photographs in this book. Every
effort has been made to credit the artists, photographers and organizations
whose work has been included and we apologize for any unintentional
omissions.

AKG, London Front Cover, Back Cover top right, Back Cover top left,
2–3, 4–5, 6 centre left, 6 top right, 7 top right, 8, 13, 22, 30–31 bottom
centre, 54–55 top centre, 71, 84, 88, 89, 91, 99, 105, 115, 118, 130, 131,
143 /Cameraphoto Epoche 128–129, 133, 141. Reprinted with the
permission of The Poetry/Rare Books Collection, University Libraries,
State University of New York at Buffalo 97 **Corbis UK Ltd** Back Cover
bottom right, /Bettmann/Library Of Congress Back Cover bottom left,
146/Bettmann 60, 61, 67 top right, 67 bottom right, 76, 125,
140/Bettmann/Library of Congress 43/Bettmann/UPI 62 centre left, 108,
117, 134, 139/Hulton Getty 7 top left, 127, 92–93/Jan Butchofsky-Houser
159 **Hulton Getty** front endpaper, back endpaper, 7 centre right, 56, 58,
59, 64–65 top centre, 69, 81, 122, 123, 124, 137, 144–145 Courtesy of
The John Fitzgerald Kennedy Library 1, 6 centre right, 6 top left, 10–11,
14, 16–17, 21, 24 bottom left, 25, 26, 28, 32, 35, 38, 40, 41, 46, 48,
50–51, 52, 53, 73, 74–75, 98, 100, 102–103, 104, 109, 120/Chapresto
Logrono 150 **Kobal Collection**/20th Century Fox 70, 86, 87/Paramount
94, 96, /Warner Bros. 107, 148, 149 **Magnum Photos** /Robert Capa 7
centre left, 110–111, 112, 114, 116, 156–157/T. Johnson 155 From the
collection of **The Ernest Hemingway Foundation Of Oak Park** 18, 19,
20, 24 top left, 29, 36, 37, 45, 47, 72, 85 **Reportage Pictures**/Osvaldo
Salas 152-153 Reproduced with permission – **Toronto Star Syndicate** 62
bottom left.